BROTHERS
OF THE
DESERT

BROTHERS
OF THE
DESERT

THE STORY OF THE MONASTERY
OF CHRIST IN THE DESERT

MARI GRAÑA

Foreword by

ABBOT PHILIP LAWRENCE, OSB

SANTA FE

Sunstone books may be purchased for educational, business, or sales promotional use. For information please write: Special Markets Department, Sunstone Press, P.O. Box 2321, Santa Fe, New Mexico 87504-2321.

Cover photograph by Jcpage Photography
Book and cover design by Vicki Ahl

Library of Congress Cataloging-in-Publication Data:

Graña, Mari, 1936–
Brothers of the desert: the story of the Monastery of Christ in the Desert / Mari Graña; foreword by Abbot Philip Lawrence.
    p. cm.
Includes bibliographical references.
ISBN-13: 978-0-86534-503-4 (softcover: alk. paper)   ISBN-10: 0-86534-503-4
1. Monastery of Christ in the Desert (Abiquiu, N.M.) —History.
2. Abiquiu (N.M.)—Church history.   I. Title.

BX2525.M66G73 2006
271'.1078952—dc22

                                                        2005036510

WWW.SUNSTONEPRESS.COM
SUNSTONE PRESS / POST OFFICE BOX 2321 / SANTA FE, NM 87504-2321 /USA
(505) 988-4418 / ORDERS ONLY (800) 243-5644 / FAX (505) 988-1025

*I*n memory of William Booker Kelly who, with his wife Susan, long ago introduced me to Christ in the Desert.

And in memory of Brother Christopher Gardner who taught me about the monk's journey.

Contents

A Word from the Abbot

*T*he year 2014 marks the fiftieth anniversary of the founding of the Benedictine Monastery of Christ in the Desert in 1964. As the Golden Jubilee of our monastery rapidly approaches, we are happy to present this volume, written by a long-time friend of ours, Mari Graña of Santa Fe, New Mexico. In this book she recounts some of the joys and sorrows, agonies and ecstasies, setbacks and accomplishments of our monastery in northern New Mexico and its dependencies in Mexico and Chicago.

Someone once said that many—maybe most—Benedictine monasteries, humanly speaking, should never have been founded, in the sense that so many begin without adequate personnel, financial resources, solid leadership, or a favorable political or religious climate. Despite one or all of these factors, numerous monasteries have come into being over the centuries, and many are still in existence. Christ in the Desert is no exception.

Founded at a time when religious vocations began to decline rapidly in the Catholic Church, established in an extremely remote, even harsh setting, with too few founders and too much work to do, Christ in the Desert has nonetheless weathered the storms. Seemingly against all odds, it has taken root, possessing today an adequate material fabric, a stable and suitably sized community of monks, and even having three other monasteries directly under its care. Each of these three monasteries, it should be pointed out, "found us" rather than we consciously choosing to establish other monasteries.

God's ways are truly mysterious, and we have tried to "rise to the occasion" of the apparent promptings of the Holy Spirit over these nearly fifty years of existence. Our late founder, Father Aelred Wall, is to be highly commended and remembered for his courageous step in establishing the Monastery of Christ in the Desert. We are most grateful to him and to all who have come temporarily or for a lifetime to form the community here.

I arrived at Christ in the Desert in 1974, when the monastery was ten years old and I was thirty years old. I got to know Father Aelred only after he retired to Mexico where he lived until his death in 1984. I have been on hand as a monk and prior, then abbot, over the last many years of the history of Christ in the Desert. Much has transpired since 1974. That doesn't mean the sailing has been smooth—far from it at times, in fact. But I feel blessed to have known our founder and been part of the Monastery of Christ in the Desert for all these years.

Fifty years of existence of a monastery might seem like a "drop in the bucket" compared to the great abbeys of Europe stretching back over a thousand years or more. Nonetheless we are "humbly proud" that Christ in the Desert has endured this long. I trust and pray that the monastery will carry on for many more decades, even centuries, and that it will continue to be an oasis in the desert, where monks and guests come to "taste and see the goodness of the Lord," as Psalm 33 puts it, always giving thanks and praise to the Maker for all the marvelous deeds he has done.

You might wonder why one of the monks didn't write this book. I would reply that there was no one I could free up for such a time-consuming work. For that I am grateful to Mari Graña for her initiative in accomplishing the task. I believe that someone other than a monk might be ideal to write an interpretive history, covering topics of interest to those outside a monastic context, presumably the majority of those reading the book.

The stories recounted in this book come from the memories of various people. As with all such accounts, there are different memories from different people. Some of the stories are not at all what I remember personally. But I am not writing this book, and I value the memories of others even when they differ from my own. Real history is filled with such differences.

This volume is partly intended to answer questions often asked of the monks. Mari has tried to keep in mind what others like herself might want to know about our life of prayer and work. She has constantly sought our advice and opinions on what she has written. It has been an enjoyable collaboration. Our thanks to Mari Graña and James Smith at Sunstone Press in Santa Fe, New Mexico for bringing this book to life.

"Never to despair of God's mercy" is one of our Holy Father Saint Benedict's admonitions to his monks. That is good advice at the beginning, middle, and end of a monastery's history. If we can all rely on God's mercy, there is nothing to fear. "May God bring us all to everlasting life," also words from the *Rule of Saint Benedict,* is the raison d'être and goal of every monastery.

I hope you enjoy this interpretive history of our monastery. Please keep us in your prayers and be assured of ours.

God bless you and all who read this book, and who have been part of the history of the Monastery of Christ in the Desert.

—Abbot Philip Lawrence, OSB

✒ 1

In the Beginning...

The basic renewal that is offered to us, that recently you held in your snow-covered hands, speaks silently, but must be heard.

—George Nakashima to Father Aelred Wall

When word reached Santa Fe that a fledgling Benedictine monastery had been founded seventy-five miles north in a remote river canyon of the high desert of New Mexico, a curious news reporter drove out the last thirteen miles of dirt track to interview the newly appointed prior, Father Aelred Wall. The reporter asked the prior if retiring to a monastery wasn't merely an escape from dealing with the problems of the outside world. Father Aelred responded, pointedly, "A monastery is not a refuge, not a solution to problems of adjustment. Monasticism is a head-on collision with reality, and the more silent, the more solitude, the more head-on it is."

The year was 1964, a time when the "outside" world seemed to be fast approaching any number of head-on collisions. The Cold War was fomenting fear of nuclear attack in all camps; conflict was occurring over the regimes in Eastern Europe, and the nations were beginning to realize the disastrous mess that unrestrained industrial development had left on the environment. In this country, protest was developing as the offensive in Vietnam escalated with the Gulf of Tonkin Resolution; some people, fearing a holocaust, were building bomb shelters in their backyards. Not only was American opinion dangerously conflicted over the war, the civil rights movement with its sit-ins, church bombings, school integration, busing and resultant armed conflict, along with the demands of the women's movement for equal pay and legal rights, were challenging our society, creating opportunities for some groups and vicious divisions within others. The year before, four little girls attending Sunday school were bombed to death in Alabama, and a few individuals decided that the murder of political leaders—beginning with President John F. Kennedy, then a few years later, the Reverend Martin Luther King and Attorney General Robert Kennedy—was the way to express their social hostilities.

The 1960s brought great changes in the Catholic world as well. In Latin America, the Liberation Theology movement charged the Church with ignoring the profound social injustices suffered by the poor; non-Catholic world opinion was pressuring Church leaders to abandon their defensive posture toward the modern world, forcing them to acknowledge the impulses toward reform that had been repressed for the last century and a half. Laity and clergy—bishops and priests, monastic leaders and their religious followers— were seeking to implement the new social and liturgical changes mandated by the Second Vatican Council.

In this context of worldwide unrest and transformation, a small Benedictine monastery in Elmira, New York determined to establish a foundation where the tenets of the simple life of prayer and work espoused by their sixth century Italian founder, Saint Benedict, could be practiced in a place of quiet and beauty, a place where the individual could seek within himself the peace and knowledge of God in a world of social upheaval and violence.

The Monastery of Mount Saviour at Elmira had existed since 1950 in a collection of rustic farm buildings, and by 1964 the brothers had only just completed the permanent construction of their rural monastery. At that time, the monastery had already some thirty-six monks plus lay assistants—far more than could be provided for—and the prior, Father Damasus Winzen, a refugee from Nazi Germany, realized that a new foundation was necessary to accommodate the increasing number of postulants seeking entry to monastic life.

Father Aelred Wall, a Benedictine monk and teacher at Rhode Island's Portsmouth Priory School, had grown tired of his administrative responsibilities as headmaster, and felt called to seek a place where he could lead a more contemplative life. He spent an extended stay with the Mount Saviour brothers at Elmira, but came to believe that a move to a Cistercian community would be more appropriate for him. Father Damasus suggested that rather than transfer his vows to a different Order, Aelred should scout the country to find a site where Mount Saviour could establish an entirely new monastery.

Father Aelred accepted this commission with enthusiasm and set out to find a suitable place for the new foundation. He searched from Maine to Michigan to Ontario, but was unable to find a location that was sufficiently remote from the busy world. On his way to California to continue his search, Aelred stopped in New Mexico to see his friend, Jerome Monks, a history professor at the College of Santa Fe. Aelred looked at several properties in New Mexico, but none of them had the seclusion that he felt was essential. Finally he heard of an old farmhouse for sale in a remote canyon in the New Mexican desert. Although it was the dead of winter, Jerome's wife, Florence, in the Monks' little Volkswagen, accompanied Aelred in his resolve to find the place. But the two had to turn back. The thirteen-mile dirt track to the farmhouse was impassible from recent snows, ankle deep with slush and mud and washed out in places. On their second attempt, however, Aelred discovered the little structure in what is one of the most beautiful canyons in the Southwest. When he saw the colorful cliffs towering over the Chama River, he was ecstatic, writing to his friends at Mount Saviour:

> Then came the cathedrals in stone, some of them Romanesque, some of them Gothic…a wide river valley with great sentinels of high, multicolored cliffs…to guard and protect it, to make it a place of God's dwelling among men. No words seem adequate to express the joy of that moment.

Father Aelred was a native of Saint Louis, and one of his Saint Louis childhood friends, Caroline Kelly, was at that time a realtor in Santa Fe. The monk asked Caroline to arrange the purchase, and the farmhouse, along with 115 acres on the floodplain and cliffs along the Chama River, was acquired by Mount Saviour for $25,000.

Surrounded by both the Carson and the Santa Fe National Forests, the peace and beauty of the remote river site was precisely what Aelred was seeking. At the canyon bottom, beneath the 500-foot rock walls of the Mesa de las Viejas, he envisioned a foundation where his followers could "return to the sources," return to the primitive life Saint Benedict had lived long ago in his cave at Subiaco. But this new Subiaco would embrace not just religious, but people of all walks and all faiths. It would be a place of quiet and beauty, where people could retreat from the clamor and insecurity of the present and seek in their hearts the peace that passes understanding. Aelred believed that the monks and guests who would come to the new monastery would "not turn their backs on the world; they would leave it to re-enter it at a deeper level."

For centuries, the desert has played an important role in the history of Christian life, particularly in Christian monasticism. Jesus went into the desert for forty days to test the strength of his will against the seductive wiles of the Devil, and the Desert Fathers sought the vast arid expanses of North Africa and Asia Minor as a place to worship, apart from the distractions of a turbulent world. Father Aelred considered the desert to be "a place where one sees the true proportion of things, a place of purification and repentance, a place where God's providence becomes unmistakably clear."

Archbishop James Davis of Santa Fe, eager to host the establishment of the new foundation in his diocese, gave his blessing to the project. Pulling a U-Haul loaded with camping equipment, several suitcases, and a cello, Father Aelred and two other monks from Mount Saviour, Father Placid Cormey and Father Basil De Pinto, along with a friend they picked up on the way, drove into New Mexico on the Feast of Saint John the Baptist, June 24, 1964.

Father Damasus' directive to Aelred had been to "find a place for primitive observance in the tradition of Saint John the Baptist." Because of the monks' opportune arrival on the feast of Saint John, the saint—another denizen of the desert—became the new foundation's spiritual father. The founding monks decided that the new monastery would be named Christ of the Desert— later changing the "of" to "in."

Father Aelred, Father Basil, and Father Placid en route to the Chama Canyon.

Beginnings...A Monastery of Tents.

The three monks, joined by visiting brothers from Mount Saviour and several lay volunteers, set up their tents along the broad bank of the Chama and began their work. They converted the four rooms of the old family farmhouse of the previous owner, Juan Gallegos, into a temporary chapel, a library/refectory, a visitors' room, and a kitchen. One of the first sacraments that Father Aelred performed in the little farmhouse chapel was the baptism of Juan Gallegos's infant grandson.

The brothers leveled twenty acres of floodplain and pumped irrigation water from the river. Despite the water running down the gopher tunnels and rat holes, they planted alfalfa, oats, and corn for the livestock. They irrigated eight hundred feet of vegetable garden and a small orchard. They built a chicken coop to house the monastery chickens, a barn for a milk cow and for Francis the mule, and permanent quarters to house the monks—four small adobe structures of two rooms each, and a fifth structure for storage and restrooms.

The Original Monks' Quarters.

Father Aelred did all the cooking in those early days, teaching in the mornings. On Sundays he would prepare a special dinner and serve beer. The monks washed their clothes by hand and hauled firewood from across the Chama in a pickup. The celebration of the Divine Office was held daily in the little farmhouse chapel, as was the Eucharist. Father Aelred introduced the Gelineau Psalter for chanting the Divine Office—the Gregorian music that the monks chant today would come much later.

The monastery's first monastic candidate, Joe Burns, dug a pond that attracted the wild ducks that frequently graced the refectory table along with fresh vegetables from the garden and bread baked by the brothers in an outdoor adobe *horno*. In addition to the wild ducks that came voluntarily, Joe brought some domestic ducks for the pond. One day, the candidate's irate family arrived at the monastery and demanded that he leave immediately; thereafter, the monks ate the domestic ducks too.

Father Aelred Blesses the Meal in the Ranch House.

The brothers of Christ in the Desert soon discovered that many friends were willing to brave the barely passable dirt road to help them. A Trappist monk, Father Denis Hines, came to the canyon to advise the brothers on the vegetable planting and care of the livestock. Father Denis built himself a tiny hermitage of fieldstone a short distance upstream from the main monastery grounds. The charming little river-edge structure of two towers, one for a chapel and one for sleeping, with views upriver to the canyon narrows and downriver to the wide, cliff-bound valley, is still used by monks seeking the eremitic life. The famous New Mexico artist, Georgia O'Keeffe, was a frequent visitor from her home at Ghost Ranch near the village of Abiquiú, and was an occasional artistic consultant on the early building progress. O'Keeffe was so taken by Brother Denis's little hermitage, that the brothers had to talk her out of moving in.

Father Denis's Hermitage.

Father Aelred brought an Airedale puppy, Brother Chico, to live at the monastery. But Brother Chico was a roamer, and the monks' work was continually interrupted in order to search for him. Sometimes Chico only got as far as Scull ranch, five miles downriver, but occasionally Aelred or one of the brothers had to drive twenty-five miles to Abiquiú to bring him back. The puppy died on one of these forays, and the brothers buried him on the grounds. Brother Chico was replaced by Padraic, an Irish setter who was always present in the ranch house chapel at the feet of his master during the daily celebrations of the Offices. But alas, Padraic, too, succumbed to the wilds of the canyon, to be replaced by a dog of unknown parentage. Over the years, many canines have kept company with the monks.

The brothers wore short denim tunics with leather belts and boots. Father Aelred, and later Father Gregory, the only solemnly professed monks, wore wooden crosses. (Much later, in 1997, the monks reverted to wearing the traditional black robe, which, during the Middle Ages, earned Benedictines the name, "Black Monks.") As was practiced at Mount Saviour, the first monastery in America to try to eliminate the category of lay brother, Aelred wanted the brothers of Christ in the Desert to be "just monks." Indeed there would be some priests among them, but aside from a priest's sacramental role in celebrating the Mass, there should be no other distinctions. There had not been hierarchical distinctions among the monks in Saint Benedict's time. Benedict, himself, was not a priest, nor were most of the monks of that period. The abbot was the father of the family, and after him, everyone else was considered of equal status. Aelred wanted to recapture that early ideal.

George Nakashima, a well-known architect and woodworker from New Hope, Pennsylvania, was a personal friend of Father Aelred. For a time, the architect had been a monk in India with the Hindu yogi, Sri Aurobindo. While studying with the famous yogi, he was contracted to design the principal disciples' residence at the Pondicherry ashram. Later he became a Catholic, and made the furniture for the monks at Mount Saviour. Nakashima understood his work as a form of prayer, as a way of coming to God. "We woodworkers have the audacity to shape timber from these noble trees," he once said. "In a sense it is…the path of action we must take to lead to our union with the Divine."

Father Aelred asked his friend to design a chapel for Christ in the Desert, but since the brothers had no money to pay for architectural services, Nakashima designed the chapel at no charge. Although no longer a monk, the architect was deeply committed to the monastic mission of love, a mission that in his personal life, he strived to achieve in the face of the political and social conflicts that were holding the world in a deathly grip. He told Father Aelred, " Your type of monasticism might be the only hope we have left, [given] the almost complete breakdown of diplomatic tact by our bumbling government. The basic renewal that is offered to us, that recently you held in your snow-covered hands, speaks silently, but must be heard."

Building the chapel was truly a community effort. Workers from the village of Abiquiú, twenty-five miles away, as well as student volunteers, came to help the brothers mix the straw and mud to make the adobe bricks and the plaster for the walls. They cut the logs for the wall supports and the roof *vigas* and the small branches for the crosspiece ceiling *latillas*. Coordination of the building process was difficult because of the remoteness of the location, with only a donated radiophone for communication to the outside. The phone radioed a motel in Chama, and, depending on whether anyone was there to answer, the message would be routed on. Nakashima initially had envisioned that the chapel would be painted white, inside and out, but when he saw the stark white of the new monks' quarters the brothers had just painted, he realized that white was a mistake. At his suggestion, the monks painted over their quarters with adobe plaster to blend in with the surroundings, and the chapel walls retained the earth tones of the natural adobe clay. The new chapel rose in the shape of a Greek cross, four one-story wings stretching out from tall central clerestory walls of glass panes. The glass captures the golden sunlight that splashes across the rugged orange cliffs that form the backdrop to the structure, bringing into the chapel the intense blue of the New Mexican sky and the stars of the desert night. Nakashima had planned to carve an altar of oak, but a Benedictine monk from Colorado offered the present altar as a gift. It is a massive stone table set in the center of the church, reminiscent of the altars in the twelfth century circular chapels of the Knights Templars. The altar is bathed in an almost surreal, numinous light from the story of windows above it. Two openings were made in the chapel walls for stained glass windows commissioned from the famous artist Ben Shahn. The hand-carved doors, a gift from a generous Santa Fe donor, were brought from Mexico. The original pews were simple logs split down the middle, and wooden crosspiece candelabras hung from the ceiling provided the lighting. The tower holds an ancient bell from a church in the northern New Mexican village of Questa, probably brought originally from Spain. Joseph Ferran of Abiquiú oversaw the construction; the cost was $25,000, a gift from Helen Wall, the prior's mother.

The chapel embodies the spirit of the land, without in any way being imitative. As one observer commented, "Neither the desert nor the monastery has been altered. Instead, each has been enhanced and beautified by the presence of the other." Thomas Merton, who visited Christ in the Desert in 1968 en route to his fateful journey to Asia, remarked in his journal: "The monastic church fits perfectly into its setting. Stark, lonely, stately in its simplicity, it gazes out over the sparse, irrigated fields into the widening valley. The bell tower is like a watchman looking for something or someone of whom it does not speak."

George Nakashima Breaking Ground for the Chapel.

George Nakashima's own words perhaps best describe his design:

"Architecture and structure are not just abstract ideas; they must relate to the environment of the building and the materials available. In a sense, a structure evolves from the materials used. I am at war with the usual architectural practice of starting with form; this is an egotistical concept, for you are left with having to fit structure into form. Here we are twenty-five miles from the next town and getting materials is a big task in itself. But we have adobe in the canyons and *vegas*, so it's natural to use them. The use of adobe affects the structure and appearance of a building. The walls have to be very thick, between three and four feet; the openings are small, and the form of the building is necessarily very different from most modern buildings with their large expanses of glass and curtain walls."

Nakashima's chapel would soon become famous as the most uniquely designed example of religious architecture in the Southwest.

Father Aelred paved the adobe floor of his chapel with Navajo rugs and weavings from the village of Chimayó. For the *nichos* in the chapel walls, the Tesuque *santero*, Ben Ortega, carved a figure of Saint John the Baptist holding a cross and a lamb, and, from a giant cottonwood log he found floating in the river, a figure of Our Lady. On Christmas Eve of 1966, Father Aelred, wearing hand-sewn vestments made by a Native American group, along with five monks, the monastery dog, and a crowd of some fifty well-wishers, celebrated Mass for the first time in the new chapel.

☙ 2

The Tijerina Affair

Whe Father Aelred was pursuing his dream of establishing, "in the tradition of Saint John the Baptist," a haven of silent work and prayer in the Chama Canyon, a violent twentieth century range war was erupting all over northern New Mexico. In 1963, a Texas-born Mexican and one-time itinerate evangelist, Reies Lopez Tijerina, along with a small band of followers, had formed the *Alianza Federal de las Mercedes*—the Federal Land Grant Alliance. The mission of the *Alianza* was to force the return of the Spanish and Mexican *mercedes* —the land grants of New Mexico—to their rightful owners, the descendants of the original grantees. The *Alianza* considered the land "usurped" and "occupied" by the takeover of New Mexico by the *Americanos.*

Tijerina had been fomenting trouble among the Hispanic population of northern New Mexico for a number of years, although resentment about the loss of grant lands had been seething in the villages for more than a century—and continues still. Since the 1930s, the Forest Service had selectively allocated permits for grazing and timber cuts on the previously owned grant lands; this was perceived by the Hispanics to favor large, mostly Anglo cattle operations and the timber industry.

There had been uprisings over the land grant issue before: in the 1880s a group called *Las Gorras Blancas* –"the White Hats"—had burned houses, cut fences, and sabotaged the track and trestles of the new railroad; and in the early 1900s, another group, *La Mano Negra*—"the Black Hand"—had terrorized Anglo owners of the former 1832 Mexican Tierra Amarilla grant lands with arson and fence cutting. The Tierra Amarilla issue erupted again more recently when, in 1963 and '64, a group calling itself the Abiquiu Corporation, a forerunner of the *Alianza*, sent hand-written eviction notices to the Anglo property owners on the grant and posted signs and armed guards at property gates. (Still today a huge hand-painted sign proclaiming *Tierra o Muerte* stands at the road edge of Highway 84 outside the village of Tierra Amarilla, twenty-five miles north of the monastery.)

In April 1963, the *Alianza* marched down the streets of Albuquerque, five hundred men, women, and children on foot and horseback, carrying banners proclaiming, "The USA is trespassing in New Mexico." The issue was the injustice of the United States' failure to respect Mexican-owned land grants guaranteed in the 1848 Treaty of Guadalupe Hidalgo that ended the Mexican-American war. The *Alianza* insisted the *merced* of San Joaquín del Rio Chama be returned to the rightful owners, the heirs of the original grantees. New Mexico's governor, David Cargo, didn't take the *Alianza* protest seriously, although one official suggested that perhaps ninety percent of Hispanic New Mexicans did indeed believe that their land had been stolen from them.

The Hispanic district attorney, Alfonzo Sánchez, was disgusted by Tijerina's exhortations, and suggested to the FBI that Tijerina was involved in Communist activities. Sánchez felt that most northern New Mexicans were more interested in the provision of roads, schools, employment opportunities, and social services, than in beating what some felt was the dead horse of the land grant issue.

If Father Aelred noticed on the title history that the Rio Arriba County property he was purchasing was once part of the *merced* of San Joaquín del Rio Chama, granted in 1808 to Francisco Salazar and thirty fellow settlers, undoubtedly he would have paid the entry scant attention. The huge grant had comprised some 473,000 acres, stretching from the Tierra Amarilla grant on the north to the villages of Capulin and Gallina on the south on what is now Highway 96; east to what is now Highway 84 and west to the Continental Divide. There were many villages within the grant area, as well as the Cañon del Rio Chama. The little settlement of San Joaquín, built on the west bank of the river near what is today the Scull Bridge, was disbanded by 1832 because of

Indian raids; the settlers moved northwest to the confluence of Gallina Creek with the Chama.

All this had taken place well in the past, and the land had long since passed into private and government ownership. Therefore, one might imagine Aelred's surprise when, in September of 1966, Reies Tijerina and some of his friends arrived at the monastery in search of the ruins of the village of San Joaquín. The monks assured their visitors that they had seen no traces of the long-defunct settlement.

The land grant issue escalated a month after the *Alianza* visit to the monastery. Tijerina and his men, three hundred fifty strong, took possession of the national forest campground at Echo Amphitheater, a large natural stone hollow on the wall of Navajo Canyon, just north of the turn-off to the monastery's dirt road. The Echo Amphitheater is located on the old San Joaquín del Rio land grant. The *valientes,* as Tijerina's supporters saw themselves, charged that the United States was occupying the peoples' land, and held a "trial" of two U.S. Forest Service rangers for "trespassing." Their intention was to challenge the purportedly illegal seizure by the U.S. of the former *ejido* lands—lands now in federal national forest, but previously owned in common by the original grantees. The Forest Service had gained possession of the common lands as a result of the 1897 Supreme Court decision (*U.S. vs. Sandoval*) in which the Court determined that common grant lands belonged to the government rather than to the individual grantees. The legality of the Court's decision has long been in question, and the insurgents demanded that the Forest Service legally prove its ownership. A standoff ended with the state police disbanding the insurgents and arresting five, including the "judge" and Tijerina's younger brother. Tijerina, although he claimed he hadn't laid a hand on the rangers, was blamed for the actions of the *Alianza* members, and would be sentenced later to a federal prison term. But first the authorities would have to catch him.

During the later months of 1966 and early '67, unseen hands cut fences, including those of the Presbyterian Conference Center at Ghost Ranch, a few miles from the monastery. Water tanks were shot up, barns, houses, and haystacks were burned, and forest fires "of suspicious origin" blazed. Vandals assaulted the Echo Amphitheatre campground and hacked up the restrooms, picnic tables, and signs.

In the early days of June 1967, American newspapers were full of events of the Arab-Israeli war. However, on June 6, a news release from New Mexico caused Americans, as the writer Peter Nabokov reported, to "hastily recheck the dateline to make sure they were still in the twentieth century."

The previous day, the *Alianza* protest had exploded in violence when a small group of supporters bearing rifles attacked the Rio Arriba County courthouse in Tierra Amarilla. The insurgents were attempting to secure the release of ten of their members jailed in the courthouse and to make a citizen's arrest on District Attorney Sánchez, who, it turned out, wasn't there. The shootout lasted almost two hours until the insurgents finally fled into the mountains, leaving one policeman severely wounded, the courthouse jailor shot twice, several state police cars shot up, a UPI reporter and a sheriff's deputy taken hostage, and a village in terror. Apparently Tijerina—who by now had been dubbed "King Tiger" by the press—was still in hiding, and didn't participate in the shoot-out.

The ensuing manhunt was the largest in the history of New Mexico. The National Guard was called out, along with police and sheriffs from the northern counties, posses official and unofficial, and the Jicarilla Apache tribal police. Helicopters and planes buzzed the mountains; tanks and jeeps searched the woods, arroyos, and every backwater that might provide cover for the fugitives. The searchers went door-to-door in the villages and countryside, and jeeps with machine guns mounted on top barricaded the county roads. To no avail. Only later were some of the fugitives arrested. Tijerina was finally caught outside Albuquerque, sleeping in a car.

While all this uproar was going on, the monks of Christ in the Desert were going quietly about their business of work and prayer, tending their vegetable garden and livestock, eating their meals in silence, and reciting the Divine Office in their new chapel. Nevertheless, the manhunt found its way to their peaceful canyon. Three heavily armed state police, wearing old khaki clothes, arrived at the monastery seeking the Tierra Amarilla insurgents. Terrified at the sight of three pistols, a rifle, and a machine gun, a shaken Father Aelred initially thought they were Tijerina's men. Finally realizing they were state troopers, he assured them that the brothers weren't harboring any fugitives. Nevertheless the police interrogated the monks and searched their quarters, along with the ranch house, the chapel, and every chicken coop and barn. At last, satisfied no one was hiding on the monastery grounds, the troopers—to the monks' great relief—got back in their cars and left.

To Father Aelred's surprise, the following Sunday the policemen returned to the canyon, this time unarmed and with their families. They had come to celebrate Mass. After the service, they pulled three bundles from the trunks of their cars: two ancient carved wooden saints and a beautiful near life-sized figure of Christ on the cross. The carving of Christ had been found in the ruins of a crumbling chapel on the New Mexico-Colorado border. The policemen told Father Aelred that these objects had been in their families for many years, but they felt that now the brothers should have them.

Father Aelred marveled how the Lord works in mysterious ways. He had the gifts repaired, and the *Cristo* hung on the wall of the chapel for many years.

Although Tijerina claimed he was not at the Tierra Amarilla shoot-out, he was again held responsible for the *Alianza's* actions. Later at the trial of the courthouse raiders—November 13-December 12, 1968—he defended himself with his usual messianic bravado: "I stand before you as David before Goliath." Eulogio Salazar, the courthouse jailor, testified, apparently falsely, that Tijerina had shot him. And for this, the jailor was later found mysteriously bludgeoned to death. Initially, sixty-four charges were brought against Tijerina and his *Alianza* followers. Ultimately Tijerina's trial was severed from that of his followers, and the charges against the leader were reduced to three, one being an illegal citizen's arrest, which turned out to be legal in New Mexico after all. Although later Tijerina indeed served time for his involvement in the Echo Amphitheater "trial" and other federal offenses, he managed to convince the jury he was innocent of the courthouse shoot-out and was acquitted. The *Alianza* was ecstatic; District Attorney Sánchez was disgusted.

⚶ 3

One Disaster After Another

Except the Lord build the house, in vain do its builders labor.

—Psalm 127

*O*ver the next years, a steady rotation of monks from Mount Saviour came to help out the new monastery. Father Aelred was determined that his monastery should become self-sufficient, but this would take longer than he expected.

There were only five monks at Christ in the Desert in 1966: Father Maur Flemming from Portsmouth Priory and Father Placid from Mount Saviour, Brother Stephan Galban, a Cuban brother also from Mount Saviour, the Trappist hermit, Brother Denis, and Father Aelred. There was also a hired man, Andronico, the brother of Juan Gallegos. Andronico and his wife, Ida, lived in a small house upriver near Brother Denis's little hermitage. Andronico helped with the garden and the animals, and his wife baked the communion wafers and bread. The two lived at the monastery during the week and returned to their home in the village of Gallina on weekends. The brothers also hired a carpenter, but unfortunately, the carpenter liked to drink; one evening he consumed an entire case of beer that Father Aelred had brought back from town for a special celebration.

Brother Stephan worked with an Indian family in a nearby pueblo to learn the basic techniques of pottery firing. He created clay angels and crosses, figures of the Holy Family, and Christmas ornaments, which he fired in the kiva fireplace in the ranch house. These he sold in the Artes Shop of the New Mexico Museum Foundation. Such an effort was helpful, but would hardly bring in the kind of money needed to support the monastery.

The prior was especially eager to build a guesthouse for the many people who wished to come for retreats. The guesthouse was an integral part of his dream to open his monastery to people of all faiths and of no faith to experience the peace and beauty of the canyon. He believed strongly Saint Benedict's dictum that a guest should be received as Christ —although donations would be appreciated.

The monks actively sought funds from the monastery's friends to build the guest quarters, but early in the winter of 1968, their plans were thwarted by near disaster. Heavy rains caused the new monks' cells to "leak like sieves." The rain bore down on the galvanized roof of the new chapel, leaking down the walls and into the earthen floor. Eighteen inches of snow created more leaks, and moisture ate into the mud plaster. The monks feared their masterpiece would collapse. The $10,000 they had to build the guesthouse wasn't even enough to pay a contractor to fix the cells, replace the chapel roof, and refinish the walls. Additionally, to the brothers' disappointment, the two openings left in the chapel walls for the stained glass windows Nakashima had commissioned from Ben Shahn, had to be sealed shut. The windows were never delivered; the artist had suffered a heart attack. For many years, the location of the filled openings could still be seen on the outside walls.

More trouble was in store for the monks. Because of a boundary dispute—a common occurrence in New Mexico, where often boundaries are at best "approximate"—the Forest Service refused to allow a cattle guard at the monastery gate or permit a water line to be built to the proposed guesthouse. The government surveyor insisted that some eighty acres that Aelred assumed belonged to the monastery were actually in the national forest. Fortunately for the brothers, two former pupils from the school at Portsmouth Priory where previously Aelred had been headmaster, William Ruckelshaus and Peter Flanagan, had high positions in the Nixon Administration, Ruckelshaus heading the new Environmental Protection Agency. Under pressure from these two, the Forest Supervisor agreed to settle title for $7,500. Of course, this meant that more funds needed to be raised.

Then in the summer, the rain was so heavy that the road washed out, leaving the monastery and its neighbors stranded. Father Aelred appealed to Governor David Cargo for funds to fix it, but the governor informed him that the road belonged to no one, and therefore state or county funds could not be used. An appeal to the Forest Service was also denied. Mt. Saviour balked at helping the monks with funds for the guesthouse until the road was repaired, so the monks were forced to fix it themselves.

Early in 1969, Father Aelred and Brother Anthony Lo Bianco traveled around the country trying to raise money to build the guesthouse. Karl Tani, an artist friend of Aelred's, had designed the tumbleweed letterhead and distinctive print that is still used by the monastery. Aelred used the new letterhead to send out an appeal for funds: "Put Christ in the Desert by Christmas" and "A Dollar a Brick will do the Trick." Ten thousand adobe bricks were needed. Finally that winter, the brothers raised enough money that a guesthouse of nine "cells"—six for men, three for women—also a Nakashima design, was under construction.

But soon the guesthouse was in trouble again. Nakashima didn't bother with formal architectural drawings—it was all "on the spot" design. Unfortunately, however, he could not be "on the spot" during the construction process, and the work was left in the hands of a builder from Albuquerque.

When the noted Santa Fe architect, Bill Lumpkins, came to the monastery for a visit, he was appalled to see the shoddy construction under way at the guesthouse. The roof wasn't properly pitched, the windowsills didn't slant away from the building, and the walls were much too thin to provide privacy in the cells. For a simple building without the need for electrical conduits and with the interiors left unfinished, Lumpkins told Aelred the $50,000 charged for the work was "simply ridiculous!" When Nakashima came to see the construction, he immediately wrote to the builder: "The workmanship is unbelievably bad. Almost any high school grad or farm boy could have done better. The portal leaks, standard doors simply cut in two to make dutch doors are unacceptable, the windows leak, the second floor handrail is hazardous, and I never heard of windows with the putty on the inside."

Of course, this plunged Father Aelred into the middle of a fight between a very defensive builder and a very unhappy Nakashima who considered the whole affair a "tragic experience." The builder threatened a lawsuit. Father Aelred wrote to him, "There was a tremendous amount of drinking at night and on the job. The building is a disaster, the loss inestimable... all the time the community has put into the work—that obviously has to be done over. There is also the loss of income from the guesthouse that we expected to be finished last spring."

The guesthouse debacle was finally settled at some expense, but at least without a lawsuit. Father Aelred lamented later in a letter to Nakashima: "Without the love of God, one could go mad in a place like this."

Father Aelred Celebrating Mass in the New Chapel; Father Gregory Assisting.

With all this turmoil, the brothers were far from achieving the contemplative life. The monks' quarters were lighted by electricity produced by a generator. Every time someone switched on a light, the generator would go into action, and the roar could be heard up and down the canyon. The machine also had a habit of kicking on all by itself in the middle of the night, waking everyone.

And there were accidents: many from construction, some from more bizarre happenings. Ed Brosseau, the property owner across the river, had put his hand into a fireplace to clean it, and a rattler, curled on the firebricks, bit him on the hand. The monks radioed the Chama motel that called the hospital in Española, and Ed was rushed—as fast as one could be rushed on the rutted road—to meet the doctor out at the highway. Ed never regained the use of some of his fingers.

Brother Anthony and three visitors climbed the Mesa Golondrina, across the river from the monastery, to search for the ruins of an Anazasi pueblo. Anthony became separated from the others, and when he tried to return to the monastery, he couldn't find the way he had come. He started to descend the cliffs, lost his footing, and started to slide. He stopped just feet from going over a sheer drop-off. He took off his boots to rest his feet, but when he tried to put the boots back on, his feet had swollen so much that he couldn't. He spent the night stuck on the ledge above the drop-off until Andronico and the state police found him and pulled him back up the cliff with a rope. Anthony had to be rescued by helicopter and taken to a hospital. It was January, and his feet were gangrenous from frostbite. He was unable to work for several weeks.

A Danish monk from Mt. Savior, Brother Ansgar Kristensen, came to help the monastery for a while. When he arrived in the canyon, he found Father Gregory the only monk, alone with three hash-smoking hippie guests. Ansgar wrote to Father Placid, who had returned to Elmira, "There were so many accidents—people stepping on nails, sticking arms through windows, high-speed trips to the hospital. The [propane] refrigerator broke down and we had to put all the meat in milk cans in the river, only to have the water get in and ruin everything. One candidate was drinking the sacramental wine, another threatened suicide. There were peculiar people wandering the canyon; one guest was a professional skydiver. Local rebels expected to take over the monastery, as they had proclaimed the canyon a free state of San Joaquín. One candidate was 'weird.' He had gone on a barefoot pilgrimage to Our Lady of Guadalupe. He had visions, and Aelred was relieved to see him go. Another arrived with some friends driving a hearse. He was a candidate for one night. He made Father Aelred take him back to civilization or he threatened to commit suicide. Poor Father Aelred!"

At one point Brother Ansgar was left alone in charge of the monastery. Father Gregory had left to spend time with his sick mother, Father Aelred was in Mexico recuperating from an illness, and Brother Anthony was still in the hospital recovering from frostbite. Ansgar had to take care of the animals, the vegetable garden, and do the cooking for five guests, who—apparently as part of their spiritual quests—were having pot parties down by the river.

Father Aelred pinned his hopes for self-sufficiency on a plan to raise goats to produce cheese for sale around the state. Georgia O'Keeffe volunteered to design a logo for the cheese that was to be called "Yerma," an archaic Spanish word meaning " a windswept, lonely place." The monks had constructed a goat barn, and by 1969, the monastery supported a herd of fifty sheep, sixty-two lambs, and fifteen Nubian goats. Through the efforts of Aenaeas, the billy goat, there were soon twelve kids, which the brothers discovered had to be bottle-fed three times a day.

Mount Saviour had sent $2,000 for the purchase of cheese-making equipment, and the brothers imported Frère Chaput from the Abbey of Saint Benoit-du-lac in Canada to teach them how to make cheese. Under the frère's guidance, the first batch of cheese was a great success, and the brothers consumed eight quarts of goat cheese.

In 1970, Father Aelred spent six months away from the monastery, which included seeking information about marketing his cheese. It soon became clear to him that his herd was much too small to provide enough milk for even a modest commercial enterprise. But his problems weren't only the size of the herd. He had gone ahead with the wood construction of the cheese-manufacturing wing of the goat barn without bothering to inquire about the legal requirements for cheese production. The New Mexico Public Health inspector arrived in the canyon and informed him that the manufacturing room had to be made of masonry with a tile surface on the interior walls. When the inspector tested the water from the cliffs that the brothers were using in the process, he informed the prior that the water was so full of minerals that marketing the cheese to the public would be illegal. And even if these problems could be overcome, the weather was too cold to allow for a sustained yield of marketable cheese.

So Aelred's dream of self-sufficiency was dashed, and the goat barn evolved into a pottery, then into monks' quarters, and finally, years later, into a tiny monastery for a group of nuns who would come to live on the property.

Not to be discouraged, the prior decided to keep investing in sheep, and for a while the brothers sold the wool and meat. But alas, shepherding proved to be a tremendous amount of work, and in the long run, not an enterprise that could support the monastery. A few years later some of the sheep were sold, and the rest of the herd ended up occupying freezers in Española. Contrary to ancient monastic strictures against eating the flesh of four-legged beasts, the monks were eating sheep for months.

While the prior and his brothers were dealing with these head-on collisions with architects and contractors, roads, weather, rattlers, and mineral water, they did not forget the real mission of the monastery—to create a place of peace and prayer. "The end of monastic life, the end of the desert," Father Aelred told his brothers, "is the death of selfishness and the triumph of love." To achieve such love is a difficult challenge under the best of circumstances. With the setbacks and stress of trying to physically build the monastery, simply finding the time to meditate on his monastic mission required of Aelred a profound faith in the spiritual purpose of the endeavor. Perhaps he had faith in the purpose, but the practical problems were overwhelming. According to the Trappist hermit, Brother Denis, early on Aelred "talked constantly of the likely collapse of the place."

Father Aelred returned from his recuperation in Mexico to pursue his mission with renewed, passionate intensity. Through these years of turmoil, the monks still considered their primary work the chanting of the Psalms of the Divine Office, as set forth in the ancient *Rule* of Saint Benedict. By this time, the chants had been newly translated into English, in accordance with the provisions of the Second Vatican Council. Faithfully at the appointed hours, the monks of Christ in the Desert, along with those guests who wished to participate, left off their construction work and agricultural activities to renew their life of prayer in the chanting of the Offices of the day.

But the large number of guests seeking to share in the monks' contemplative life was beginning to be a problem. Although the guests were enlisted to help with the construction and with other maintenance duties of the monastery, their presence did indeed interfere in the spiritual life of the brothers. Brother Rafael, a member of an active religious order who came to stay with the brothers for a time, recalled this conflict in a letter sent some years later to the monks. He describes the unity and love, the joyful simplicity of the life at the monastery, as well as the monks' saving sense of humor about their trials. But he also had his criticisms: "I thought we were too 'open' to the guests and visitors. The monastic sharing became a burden, at least for me. The community was too small to take on such a task. There were always guests, and since the guesthouse wasn't ready, these persons were with us continually. Then there were occasions when people dropped in for tours. This necessitated stopping our work and taking them around. In a phrase, we lacked communal privacy. During the summer, people came to picnic at various sites close by. I found this rather disturbing, and I made it known to Father Aelred. Add to that, the financial status of the monastery wasn't stable."

Yet despite the problems the guests created, Father Aelred continued firmly in his conviction that the prayerful life of the monastery should be open to a spiritually hungry world. To achieve this, he not only encouraged individual retreatants seeking spiritual renewal, he extended this welcome to families as well. In the early seventies, three families settled on the monastery grounds. Priscilla and Bob Bunker came with their children and built the "Gatehouse" at the entrance to the monastery, which at that time was closer to the river. (The Bunker house later became a weaving shop and then a hermitage. Precariously close to the water, it was demolished in 2004.) If the family was a distraction to some of the monks, it is hard to imagine how they would have survived without their help. In 1970 the convento was under construction, and Bob Bunker helped the workers. Priscilla took over managing the guesthouse when it was finally completed and did the cooking for the guests. She also fed the entire work crew, which numbered fifteen to twenty a day. There were fresh eggs, vegetables, and milk, but everything else required a shopping trip to Española.

The second family was the Richardsons, Michael and his pregnant wife, Amy. Mike had asked Father Aelred if the two could live on the grounds and work for $35 a month for him, $30 for Amy. To Mike's surprise, Aelred agreed. Amy baked all the bread for the monastery and helped Priscilla in the guesthouse; Mike worked in the alfalfa field and vegetable garden and with Bob and the construction crew on the convento. Mike had originally thought he would have time to write—he greatly miscalculated the amount of work involved for the $35. The monks built a small house for the Richardsons to the north in the vicinity of the old goat barn.

The Lang family, Friedl and Martha and their children, joined the other two families in the summer and for Friedl's six-month sabbatical from his job as professor of anthropology in Boulder. The Langs didn't build their own house, but lived first in a large tent by the river, then for a six-month stay in the Gatehouse after the Bunkers left, and later during another year, in the ranch house. Friedl worked for the brothers as an all-around handyman, fixing leaks in the chapel and guest house, building the bookshelves for the library, repairing the erratic water pump and the temperamental bathrooms, tinkering with the generators, and helping with the continuous problem of rescuing people stuck on the muddy road. After the death of Martha, Friedl joined the community in 2005 as a claustral oblate. As Brother Benedict, he now makes the monastery his home.

Father Aelred's interest in having families living on the grounds was to test the idea of a lay community beside the monastery. The idea had been suggested by Thomas Merton, who had advised the prior that he should have families living around the monastery as is common in Tibet. The three families eagerly endorsed his idea, and envisioned a lay village of some fifteen houses on the flat area inside the monastery gate. Amy Richardson wrote years later that she thought the plan was Father Aelred's alone, and that he never really discussed it with the monks. She characterized Father Aelred in her letter: "He felt he was a sculptor, and the monastery was his piece of clay. He was a visionary and made surroundings of great beauty, but was not a great leader because his ideas were not integrated with action. He was a dreamer, a very difficult person to live with—impetuous, warm, creative, but not at peace with himself, and not wise. He was so wrapped up in his own plans, ideas, and struggles over work, that he wasn't sensitive to other people." When her baby was born, Amy says Aelred seemed surprised, as if the thought of an infant living at the monastery had never occurred to him.

Amy's husband, Mike, added in a letter: "The community had a tentative, experimental nature. It had no commonly agreed on definition of itself, and this led to tension over wanting to be a contemplative community and the need to provide hospitality to an almost constant stream of visitors. This will always be a problem, but when there is no clear definition, it can verge on the impossible."

Priscilla Bunker commented recently that Father Aelred was so open to allowing people to stay that once she saw the whole alfalfa field covered with the cars of hippies. And when the activist priest, Daniel Berrigan was on the run from the F.B.I. for destroying draft registration files in Catonsville, Maryland, Father Aelred offered him sanctuary. Berrigan was caught by the authorities before he could take him up on the offer.

The winter of 1971–72 was unbearably cold—minus 30 degrees for a week. The Bunkers had gone back home to Santa Fe; the Richardsons, to keep a little warmer, were staying upstairs in the guesthouse. The few monks closed the monastery for a month and headed south, leaving Mike and Amy alone to look out for the place.

4

The Chama Canyon

The ancient weathered cliffs of the Chama Canyon are the result of sediments laid down 220 million years ago, a period of the earth's genesis that geologists call the Permian Age. At that time, the area was low, covered by tidal pools of the ancient sea that spread over much of what is now New Mexico. Gradually the canyon walls began to lift and then erode. During the next forty million years, the land was wet and humid, with shallow lakes, streams, and forests. From this time, we find petrified trees and traces of dinosaur and early mammal fossils. One of the ancient reptiles left its tracks just north of the monastery, and the crocodile-like, thirty-foot phytosaur, as well as the smaller aetosaur, which resembles a cross between a crocodile and an armadillo, left their skeletons for the paleontologists to discover.

Over the next several million years, the land continued to rise and erode, and the weather fluctuated from dry to humid. Some hundred million years ago a great ocean flooded the entire Southwest, leaving marine deposits (the Dakota formation). As the cliffs rose, the deposits, offset along fault lines, were lifted up the canyon walls. Today, these deposits have mostly eroded away, but the various formations of rock laid down over the ages have created the colorful striations of dusty orange, varnished by maroon, purple, and gray—the articulated cliffs capped with the hard, off-white Dakota limestone layer that we see along the road to the monastery.

The Chama River.

The canyon floor is home to raccoons, skunks, squirrels, porcupines and foxes, and in the river we can occasionally find a beaver-hewn log floating among the many species of fish. Over it all hover golden eagles, hawks, owls, vultures, and in winter, the American bald eagle. For a while military jets flew over the canyon as well, disrupting the prayers in the chapel, until one of the guests took it upon herself to contact the *politicos* to put a stop to the low-flying sorties.

The large canyon a quarter mile or so below the monastery gate is named for General José María Cháves, one of the original 1808 grantees of the San Joaquin del Rio Chama *merced*. General Cháves fought for the Union in the Civil War and lived to be a hundred and one. If we walk up General Cháves's canyon, (now spelled Chavez Canyon) we leave the riparian cottonwoods and willows behind and enter a steep landscape of piñon, sagebrush, and juniper. On climbing up the canyon walls to the Mesa de las Viejas, we find a covering of ponderosa pine, oakbrush, currant, serviceberry, and mountain mahogany. This is the haunt of elk, black bear, muledeer, turkey, badger, and an occasional cougar. Bears don't necessarily stay on top the mesa, however, as Brother Marcelo discovered when he found one in the refectory kitchen, enticed by the smell of pizza baking in the monastery oven. It was apparently the same bear that climbed in the window of Brother Luis's cell as Luis made a fast exit out the door. The bear pulled the sink off the wall, then went through the cupboards until it discovered Luis's secret cache of candy bars. After several unsuccessful attempts, the Forest Service finally enticed the bruin into a cage and carted him off to the wilds of Colorado. Some years later, Brother Hugh awoke one morning to find that another of the burly creatures had destroyed his beehives, tossing them all over the meadow in its quest for honey.

The monks of Christ in the Desert are among only the most recent human inhabitants of the Chama Canyon. According to the Forest Service *Chama River Canyon Wilderness Guide*, archaeologists have found projectile points in the canyon dating from as long ago as 9,500 years B.C.E., the period of the earliest recognized evidence of Paleo-Indian occupation in North America (9500 to 5000 B.C.E). Ancient pit houses, indicating possible winter occupation, have been found dating from around 3100 B.C.E. Certain types of pottery shards, chipped stone knives, and antler tools, as well as traces of storage structures, surface houses, and the stone towers unique to the Puebloan Gallina culture, indicate the Gallina peoples appeared in the canyon from 1100- 1275 C.E. There are signs that the later Puebloan Period culture overlapped with the 1540 arrival of the Spanish in New Mexico. Navajo, Ute, and Comanche peoples lived in the canyon until Spanish settlers began to move into the area, the first arriving in the late 18th century.

There was considerable conflict between the Indians and the Spanish, and the little 1808 canyon settlement of San Joaquín, established on land that is now known as the Scull Ranch, was abandoned after twenty-five years. Along with the Indian raids, the lack of adequate water for crops on the riverine terraces prompted the canyon settlers to move five miles north to another village that had been established at Gallina Creek. However, with the establishment of homesteads in the area at the beginning of the 20th century, there is scant trace now of these early 19th century habitations, or at least Father Aelred knew of no traces when Reies Tijerina and his men arrived in the canyon to ask him about the villages.

During the late19th and early 20th centuries, the settlements scattered along the river were known as "Chama Arriba." Later, the area was called "Burns Canyon." T.D. Burns, known to the area settlers as "El Bornes," was an Irishman who came as a child with his parents to the United States. He migrated from New York to Wisconsin to Colorado, and finally, in 1865, to New Mexico, where he opened a store in Los Ojos, one of the villages on the Tierra Amarilla land grant. Burns married Josefa Gallegos of Abiquiú, the daughter of a territorial legislator and niece of an early representative to the U. S. Congress. Josefa's father owned all of the Piedra Lumbre land grant, which included the village of Abiquiú, the area that is now the Ghost Ranch, and some of the lower Chama. Burns and his family settled in the village of Las Nutrias— the name of which was later changed to Tierra Amarilla.

The former state historian, Robert Torres, notes that T. D. Burns " is not remembered with affection." Many of the Hispanic settlers in northern New Mexico owed Burns for purchases they had made at his Los Ojos store and often were forced to pay their accounts with land. According to Torres, in one month alone, Burns acquired 42,000 acres. Bob Trujillo of Abiquiú, a descendent of the Gallegos family, reports that Josefa's brother, Tomás Gallegos, was for a time the priest at Abiquiu. Tomas was later excommunicated for his shady dealings with his brother-in-law.

The Rio del Chama grant, which includes the present site of the monastery, comprises only 1422 acres. It was an area set aside for the settlers living along the river when the common lands of the 473,000-acre San Joaquín grant were declared public domain by the Supreme Court in 1897—a decision that, according to some legal historians, as well as the Tijerina insurgents and the grantee heirs, was in conflict with the tenets of international law regarding ownership of commonly held grant lands.

The San Joaquín grant is another in the sordid legal history of New Mexican land grants. Although U. S. Surveyor General Proudfit recommended confirmation of the grant to the legal heirs in 1872, Congress took no action on the claim. According to historian Malcolm Ebright, land speculators were buying up parts of the grant in the 1880s.

Even while the grant was still in adjudication as to ownership, William Blakemore, a speculator who had purchased some of the parcels, was trying to sell the whole grant in England, even though he didn't own all the interests in it and didn't even know its actual size.

The heirs of the small Rio de Chama grant—that 1422-acre portion of the large San Joaquín grant that the Court set aside for the people living in the river canyon—were too poor to apply for it. Many of them were in debt to Burns or already had had to give up their land to him; in 1905 the Court awarded the patent for the smaller grant along the river to Burns.

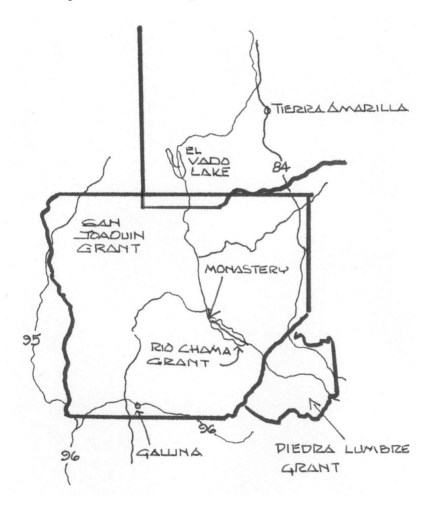

Map of the San Joaquín Grant.

Even after the Tijerina insurgents' aborted attempt in the 1960s to force the U. S. government to prove the legality of its claim to the large, 473,000-acre San Joaquín grant, in July 1979, the heirs of the grant set up a roadblock to stop logging trucks from hauling timber from the Santa Fe National Forest—from what were once grant lands. As a result of this conflict, Congressman Manuel Lujan introduced a bill in Congress to establish a commission to study the ownership claims, but the bill died in committee.

The land grant controversy still simmers. At the request of New Mexico's congressional delegation, the U.S. General Accounting Office issued a report in 2004 concluding that during the nineteenth century hearings, the government had afforded New Mexican land grant heirs due process in its consideration of their claims; hence Congress has no legal obligation to address the issue. However the GAO report acknowledges that the confirmation process had indeed created hardship for the heirs and proposes options that Congress could consider—ranging from a mere apology, to a trust fund or cash payments, to the transfer of certain national forest and BLM lands to the claimants. While many of the land grant activists prefer the last option, the transfer of public land to private ownership is extremely controversial in the state, and to date no decisions have been made.

T. D. Burns established a sheep ranch in the canyon and built an elegant adobe house on the western bank of the river, across from what is now Scull Bridge. He seldom stayed in the house, however; a foreman lived there and managed the sheep operation. After Burns' death in 1916, his grandson, Roy Hall, took over the ranch. Hall was state treasurer in 1917-18. According to notes in the monastery archives from Roy Hall's granddaughter, Marguerite Claffey of Santa Fe, Hall and the warden of the state penitentiary decided to grow beans on the ranch for the war effort. For this, they needed to widen the road into the canyon to carry trucks. The state prisoners built the road, plowed the fields, and planted the beans. No beans ever grew, but the canyon got a somewhat better road.

In the early 20th century, members of the Gallegos, Trujillo, Piña, Archuleta, and other families established homesteads in the western canyons that drain into the Chama. Since T.D. Burns owned much of the river frontage, these homesteaders did not have access to Chama water and were dependent on dry farming, which was difficult in the best of weather conditions. Some of the settlers were too poor to pay the $2.50/acre homestead price to the Forest Service, so they just lived there anyway, and the government paid them little attention. Between 1969 and 1976, the Forest Service bought back the homesteads, most of which by that time were abandoned.

Manuel and Ascencion Gallegos raised their eight children on the farm that is now the Sebastian ranch up the Gallina Canyon, beyond Burns's grant, where there was good spring water. Manuel built a wagon road (no longer passable) that led up to the town of Llaves, from where there is a road to Gallina village on Highway 94. The Gallegos children attended the little *jacal* schoolhouse that was located where Gallina Creek flows into the Chama at the edge of the monastery boundary. Juan, one of the sons, built the ranch house now owned by the monastery, where he raised his family along with sheep, cows, turkeys, and chickens. His brother, Andronico, helped Juan at the ranch caring for the animals. Another son, Julio, married into the Archuleta family. He homesteaded 177 acres five miles further up Gallina Canyon, beyond his parents' place. Manuel's brother Francisco and his sister Ursula each had a house along the western terrace of the Chama south of Gallina Creek. When Manuel died and the Gallina farm was left to his children, Juan bought out his siblings and took over the property, which he later sold to Fred and Elizabeth Berry, and which is now the Sebastian farm. Andronico hired on as Father Aelred's foreman at the monastery farm.

Guy Scull, an Easterner who settled in the canyon, bought the entire 1422-acre Rio de Chama grant, which included the large adobe house that originally had belonged to T.D. Burns. The house had passed through several hands since the Burns family owned it. Scull remodeled it and pastured cows on the river terrace, but when he died, soon after the monastery was established in the 1960s, the house was left abandoned, and the cows moved in. The Forest Service acquired the property and tore the house down, concerned that someone might get hurt climbing around in the old place.

Another relic of times past is the small adobe ruin overlooking the river to the left as the road leaves the broad, sage-covered Llano del Vado and enters the river canyon. Locally known as the "Casa de los Ingleses," the ruin was once a lookout belonging to an English company that owned livestock in the canyon in the early 20th century.

The road into the canyon, now designated Forest Service Road 151, ends at the monastery, and the road on the west side of the river from Scull Bridge to the Sebastian farm is no longer passable farther into the Gallina Canyon. Several miles upriver from the monastery, some newer houses have been built on private property across from the confluence with the Rio Cebolla.

The houses take access from the west, by 4-wheel drive road coming into the canyon from the village of Llaves. North of Cebolla Canyon, the only structure on the river until the area around El Vado Dam is the abandoned Ward Ranch, once the hideout of thieves.

With the exception of the ranch house on the monastery property, there are only traces of the early "Chama Arriba" settlements of fifty to a hundred years ago. The schoolhouse is now in ruins; Reyes Archuleta's house, later bought by Ed and Roberta Brosseau for a guest ranch, slid into the river during a flood, as did the little house of Ursula Gallegos, a mile or so downriver. Luis Trujillo's 1912 homestead in the Cañada de las Fuertes still has standing walls, but the roof is gone. Luis and his wife Selsa moved to a ranch near Abiquiu in the 1930s. Only remnants remain of Cipriano Piña's log cabin and *jacal* outbuildings in the Cañada de la Presa, although Cipriano's son, Arturo, lived at the homestead until World War II. The swinging footbridge that crossed the Chama at the mouth of Gallina Creek collapsed in a flood, as did the old bridge that gave access to the Burns ranch before the new Scull Bridge was built. Karl Bode, the former owner of Bode's general store in Abiquiú, remembers that driving the old bridge, which had no sides and was hung from cables, was an adventure. When a car or truck crossed to the middle of the river, the bridge would start to swing dangerously from the motion of the vehicle. According to the Forest Service, for a while there were still parts of old Model T's lying in the river where the bridge once was.

Manuel Gallegos's house no longer stands, replaced by a newer one on the Sebastian farm. The rest of the houses are now just melting piles of adobe bricks and heaps of *barillas*—the wooden supports used for *jacal* construction. Across Scull Bridge, the little cemetery with its wooden crosses still exists at the far edge of the river's western terrace; it contains the resting places of some of these early inhabitants.

🌿 5

The Holy Rule *of Saint Benedict*

*Listen carefully, my
son, to the master's
instructions, and
attend to them
with the ear of your
heart.*
—Saint Benedict,
Prologue to the
Rule for Monks.

The Benedictine monastery of Christ in the Desert, as
are many monastic communities, is governed by the *Regula
Sancti Benedicti*, Saint Benedict's *Rule for Monks*. The Italian
saint's "little rule for beginners," as he called his treatise,
was written almost 1500 years ago, in times far different
from ours, but perhaps no less turbulent. Barbarians from
the north sacked Rome twice in the 5th century, and the
last emperor, Romulus Agustulus, was deposed four years
before Benedict's birth. During his lifetime (c.480-547)
Benedict lived under the tenuous peace of the Ostrogoth
ruler, Theodoric, but after Theodoric's death, there was
constant war as the barbarian tribes continued to invade
the peninsula.

Perhaps it was precisely that the Roman world was
going to pieces that Benedict sought to instill a form
of order in monastic life—order that in the greater,
disintegrating society was being destroyed by war and
the corrupt autocrats of the political arena. Furthermore,
Christian monasteries had been in existence for only two
centuries, and although these early communities produced
some of the greatest monks of Christendom —the Desert
Fathers Antony and Pachomius, as well as Basil, and
later John Cassian, who introduced the rules of Eastern
monasticism to the West—still, many of the monasteries

were often little more than refuges for social misfits, peasants who had no place else to go, political malcontents, and "heretics" from Church orthodoxy as it had been determined by the council at Nicaea in 325.

We do not know if Benedict intended his *Rule* to be used beyond the institutions that he himself founded—no doubt he would be amazed to know that his little rule for beginners would guide the structure of monachism for the next fifteen centuries. But certainly he realized the need to bring order to contemporary monastic life, to present a definite statement of purpose for the institution, as well as a standard of conduct for the individual members.

Aside from the "Life and Miracles of Saint Benedict," written several years after the good saint's death, and attributed to Pope Gregory the Great as part of his *Dialogues*, we know little about Benedict's life. What we do know is that he was from Nursia, a village in northern Umbria, and that he attended school in Rome. Paganism was still prevalent in the capital at that time, and Benedict fled the city to worship his Christian God in a village near Mount Affile. From there, the fame of his miracles forced him to flee again, this time to seek seclusion as a hermit in a cave near the town of Subiaco. Pope Gregory's "Life" of Benedict is long on miracles and short on facts, but it does tell us that a group of monks from the monastery at Vicovaro entreated the saint to abandon his cave and join them as their abbot. Benedict reluctantly acquiesced to their request, but soon his stern discipline antagonized the monks. He returned to Subiaco to guide other monks in their journey to God, and in time a colony of several small monasteries developed there. The Subiaco colony well established, Benedict and some of his disciples moved on to form a new monastery. He chose a site on Monte Cassino—the mountain that looms over what, in Benedict's day, was the impoverished and largely still pagan village of Casinum. The mountain and the shrines in the forest around it were still used for sacrifices to the ancient Roman gods—in those troubled times, the village inhabitants persisted in their pagan beliefs for security against the disintegration of the society around them.

The 8th century monk and poet, Mark of Monte Cassino, suggests that Benedict established his monastery on the site of these ancient shrines in order to destroy them, and to evangelize the peasants of Casinum. Whether or not this is true, the monastery on the mountain survived beyond Benedict's lifetime until, in 581 it, too, was sacked by the barbarian Lombards. The monks of Monte Cassino fled with their sacred document to Rome, where the *Rule* was kept until the monastery was restored in the early 8th century by those same Lombardi tribes that had previously destroyed it. We do not have an original manuscript of the *Rule*; the oldest copy dates from the early 9th century, the *Codex Sangallensis* from the monastery at Sankt Gallen in Switzerland.

Shortly before the Lombards' restoration of Monte Cassino, some of the saint's relics were supposedly removed to the Gallic Abbey of Fleury, where they became the object of veneration for pilgrims during the Middle Ages. Benedict's Monte Cassino survived other attacks as well as a disastrous earthquake in the 14th century, but was finally reduced to rubble by allied aerial bombardment during the Second World War. The tombs of Saint Benedict and his sister, Saint Scholastica, miraculously were not destroyed in the bombardment. In the 1950s, the Italian government constructed an exact replica of the famous monastery, paid for partly by the United States.

In the early 9th century, Louis the Pious, son of the Holy Roman Emperor, Charlemagne, decreed that the *Rule* would be the standard of organization for all monastic institutions throughout the empire. And thus it remained the guide of monastic life through the ensuing centuries—surviving the Reformation, the dissolution of the English monasteries, the disastrous Catholic-Protestant Thirty Years' War, and the French Revolution and its subsequent waves of secular suppression in the countries of northern Europe. By the beginning of the 19th century, after a glorious history as the repositories of Western law, science, art, and learning—Monte Cassino being one of the greatest of these—the European monasteries, considered by these secular governments as worthless obsolete relics, were reduced to a mere handful, and the few monks who attempted to live by the *Rule* in these countries were looked upon as underground subversives.

Yet Benedict's *Rule* and its call to prayer, work, and love of humanity survived these political, military, and ecclesiastical assaults. It became, once again, an integral part of the revival of monasticism later in the 19th century—as we may experience today in this community of brothers who devote their lives to its precepts in the canyon of the Rio Chama.

Presumably, Saint Benedict wrote his *Rule for Monks* while he was abbot of Monte Cassino. His was not the first rule for monasteries, but it was the most concise and comprehensive. The treatise addresses both practical and liturgical matters, regulating most aspects of life in the monastery, a place that he calls a *schola Dominici servitii*—a school for the Lord's service. Benedict believes that each monastery should be autonomous and self-sustaining. The monks should consider themselves a family, subject to a strong, yet merciful abbot, much as the Roman family of his time was subject, unquestionably, to the father. The saint considers the Divine Office—the chanting of the Psalmody—as the *Opus*

Dei, the work of God, to be the primary activity of the monks. He stipulates which Psalms should be said or sung daily at each of the seven Offices and at the night Office of Vigils (although he cautions that "No one should presume to read or sing unless it benefit the hearers"). He insists the oratory, or chapel, be reserved only for prayer, and that nothing should be stored in it. He discusses the sleeping arrangements—the monks should sleep in their clothes in order to be able to rise early, but should remove their knives "lest they accidentally cut themselves in their sleep." He describes what the monks should wear ("in summer a tunic will suffice, in winter a woolen cowl is necessary, in summer a thinner or worn one; a scapular for work, and sandals and shoes.") However, the abbot must be concerned about the measurements of these garments "that they not be too short, but fitted to the wearers." He describes the food the monks may eat: two kinds of cooked food plus fruits and vegetables, but no meat from four-legged animals. He reluctantly concedes that the monks will insist on their daily half-bottle of wine, but if a monk is continually late for a meal, "let his portion of wine be taken away." He addresses the importance of work: "When they live by the labor of their hands, as our fathers and the apostles did, then they are really monks." Holy reading—*lectio divina,* a prayerful reading of the Scriptures—is prescribed for specific hours daily.

The monk must confess his errors both to the abbot and to the community: "If someone commits a fault while at any work—in the kitchen, in the storeroom, in serving, in the bakery, in the garden, in any craft, or anywhere else"—he must answer for it. If a mistake is made in the oratory—in the responsory refrain or reading—the errant one "must make satisfaction before all." Failing to do so, "he will be subjected to more severe punishment.... Children, however, are to be whipped for such a fault." (Fortunately for the children, today, a candidate must be at least twenty-two before a monastery will consider his vocation.)

Guests are to be welcomed as Christ, "by a bow of the head or by complete prostration of the body....The abbot shall pour water on the hands of the guests, and the abbot with the entire community shall wash their feet." Strict as the observance of the *Rule* is at Christ in the Desert, so far no guests have reported the guestmaster prostrating himself at their arrival, or the abbot washing their feet. Clearly some modifications have been made to the saint's regulations.

Perhaps the most controversial dicta of the *Rule* are Benedict's strictures on dealing with conflict among the brothers. Father Aelred had something to say about this as he contemplated the life of the monks who would come to this remote New Mexican canyon. Aelred had been a monk for many years in other monastic communities before founding Christ in the Desert, and he was well aware that at times there would be trouble among the members. "A monastic community is a society as any other, " he once told a reporter, "and is not immune to anger and resentment. There can be loneliness and insensitivity, even cruelty. And the unhappiness of one of its members in this tightly woven society can easily become the unhappiness, anger, or resentment of everyone in the community. Anger can strike at the roots of their faith, at the value of the difficult work they have determined to accomplish, especially under the difficult conditions they have chosen to live. Such attitudes may perhaps be displaced or mitigated in a city, where one can drink it off or distract oneself at the movies or the shopping mall. Here you can't dodge the problem—you must face it down."

Certainly, the atmosphere of silence, of chanting the Psalms—many of which address precisely those human frailties that are the cause of strife—go far in helping a disgruntled monk deal with his problems. Still, if anger persists, it must be dealt with; no society is immune to the frailties of man.

Even the saintly Benedict, who reluctantly left his cave at Subiaco to become the abbot for a group of monks, was not immune to strife in his monastery: the recalcitrant group of brothers at Vicovaro tried to poison him. This may be a reason why that holy man was adamant in his *Rule* concerning the treatment of troublemakers: "A brother guilty of a serious fault is to be excluded from both the table and the oratory. No other brother should associate or converse with him at all....Let him take his food alone in an amount and at a time the abbot considers appropriate for him. He should not be blessed by anyone passing by, nor should the food that is given to him be blessed." Benedict goes on to say that if the miscreant lacks understanding of the seriousness of his transgression "let him undergo corporal punishment."

Although Proverbs 29:19 advises *the fool cannot be corrected with words,* in a modern American monastery, corporal punishment would be downright illegal. However, the ostracization that Benedict advocates is an extremely powerful tool and can be put to use should the situation call for such an extreme. Fortunately, at Christ in the Desert, such treatment is seldom necessary. The mission of the brothers is love: love of each other, love of the whole world, love of God. This is the mission they have taken upon themselves, and if a brother considers the gratification of his ego—whatever the provocation—superior to that mission, he had best change his attitude—or leave. Benedict quotes from a letter of Saint Paul to the Corinthians: *Banish the evil one from your midst...lest one diseased sheep infect the whole flock.*

Saint Benedict is particularly concerned about the character of the abbot. The abbot is to be elected by his brothers—a most democratic idea at the time of the disintegrating Roman Empire. The criteria for election are "goodness of life and wisdom in teaching." He must be "chaste, temperate, and merciful" and he must "hate faults but love the brothers." Above all, he must rule in fairness and in love, and yet humbly acknowledge his own frailties.

Benedict recognizes the need for the individual abbot to use his own discretion regarding observance of the *Rule,* allowing adaptation to local environments and customs. And certainly modern monachism has needed to make adjustments to some of the strictures set down nearly 1500 years ago. A guest's feet are no longer washed, the whips have long been put aside, and little boys are no longer left off at the monastery gatehouse for the monks to raise. There is no old porter (Benedict insists the porter must be old, too old to "roam about") at the open gate to Christ in the Desert.

Although the *Rule* provides both spiritual and practical guidance for the monks, it is not the only directive for Benedictine monastic life. In the 15th century, several monasteries had joined together to form the Cassinese Congregation. The Congregation promulgated its own standards of monastic behavior for its members, which elaborated and further defined the requirements of the *Rule.* Much later, in response to the 19th century renewal of monasticism, several communities broke off from the Cassinese Congregation and, in 1872, formed the Congregation of Subiaco, to which Christ in the Desert belongs. For the members of the Subiaco Congregation, the *Rule* remains the teacher, especially in the liturgical practice of the Divine Office. However, Benedict's prescriptions that do not accord with the modern outlook of the Church are supplemented and interpreted by the Constitution of the Congregation. The Constitution, revised in the 1980s in accordance with the new Code of Canon Law of the Catholic Church, provides an administrative superstructure that has authority under an Abbot President to determine such things as the conditions for acceptance into the Congregation, the general qualifications for abbot, the admission of candidates, the requirements of the novitiate, transfers from one monastery to another, and terms of dismissal. Women's communities as well as those of men are included in the Subiaco Congregation. The Congregation is further broken down into Provinces that oversee, in the form of a periodic canonical Visitation, the conditions in specific monasteries. The members of the Province elect the Visitor; he must be a priest, at least thirty years old, and solemnly professed for a minimum of five years. The Visitor, generally with the assistance of one or more Co-Visitors, makes his Visitation usually every three years, and interviews everyone in the community from the abbot down to the greenest novice. He observes the workings of the monastery—the conduct of the liturgy, the manner in which the *Rule* is followed, the reception of guests, the concerns of each individual, and receives any complaints. A report is given to the monastery and also sent to the Abbot President, and any decrees that result from the Visitor's recommendations become binding on the monastery.

In 1983, the brothers of Christ in the Desert voted to join the Subiaco Congregation, and later that year the monastery was admitted to the English Province. The Visitation reports have been favorable, but one suggestion that did descend from on high was to have rice available at every meal. This was an answer to prayers—a great relief to the Asian brothers.

In addition to all this administrative governance, there is yet one more elaboration of Saint Benedict's *Rule:* the Customary. At Christ in the Desert, the Customary addresses the schedule of daily activities at the monastery: the specific times for study, for work, for meals; the times of classes for novices, for choir practice, for chapter meetings; the clothing or vestments to be worn at Eucharist, at the "Little Hours" of Terce, Sext, and None, at Vespers, Compline, Vigils, and Lauds, and the ritual conduct during the Offices. The Eucharist is not scheduled in the *Rule*. At Christ in the Desert the Eucharist is celebrated daily at the time the morning Office of Prime would be sung, hence the monastery decided not to hold this morning Office, but the Psalms that the *Rule* prescribes for Prime are spread throughout the three "Little Hours."

The Customary sets out the days for shopping trips and the amount of money budgeted for meals, behavior during times away from the monastery, access to the computers, the telephone, and visits to or from a monk's family. After all this, the Customary even allows time for a monk to be left alone: on the first Friday of every month, each member of the community takes a "Desert Day," a day spent in solitude either in his cell, on a lone walk, or perhaps on a ride on one of the monastery horses.

The monastery community is a monk's primary family. This does not mean he severs all relations with his family of birth; he may call and visit his parents and relatives at prescribed times. But on becoming a monk, he gains a new family, and thereafter he will live only in the monastery for the rest of his life. At his death, he will be buried in the monastery cemetery among his brothers who have gone before him. For thirty days thereafter, a place will be set for him at the monastery table in remembrance. In 2003 the brothers experienced the first death of one of their own. Although there are several graves and memorial crosses in the little monastery cemetery, these belong to various friends and associates. They do not belong to the monks of Christ in the Desert; Brother Christopher's grave is the first.

If a brother determines the cenobitic life in this *schola Dominici servitii* is not for him, he is not beaten, as Saint Benedict advises. The Customary states he will be given a one-way ticket to wherever he needs to go, and a thousand dollars—two thousand if he is solemnly professed—to put in his pocket.

Despite these administrative concessions to modernity, the patterns of daily life in the monastery—the Divine Office and the particular Psalms to be chanted, the stricture of *ora et labora*—prayer and work—the silence at meals and after Compline, the requirement of obedience to the superior, the regulations regarding food and the readings during meals, the renunciation of personal property, and especially the admonition to love one another—still adhere to the ancient guiding tenets of the *Rule* set down by the holy Benedict centuries ago. These are the tenets by which the brothers of Christ in the Desert seek to honor the presence of God—in their hearts, in their prayers, and each in the comportment of his daily life.

✥ 6

The Benedictines in America

The more you distance yourself from the world, the more the world will seek you out.

—Origin unknown

*T*he impulse behind the founding of the Monastery of Christ in the Desert should be considered in the broader context of Benedictinism in the United States. Since the early beginnings of the Benedictine movement in this country—around the middle of the 19th century—American monasteries were faced with far different circumstances than were the traditional, more contemplative European houses that had spawned them. America was still a frontier society, and the American Catholic Church, both parochial and monastic, was called to administer to Catholic immigrant groups and to evangelize among the Native American populations. Hence the first monastic houses focused on missionary outreach, looking to the spiritual needs of society. This thrust was not without conflict for some of the members: not all American Benedictine monks and nuns were interested in missionary activities, many desiring a more contemplative life. This conflict over the purposes of monastic life continued as the monasteries expanded westward across America, answering the call of their own version of manifest destiny.

American-born members brought different values to the communities as the older, European monks began to die off or return to their home countries. Imbued at once with both the pragmatism and the idealism of 19th century American society, as well as a very "American" sense of personal independence, many religious developed a missionary zeal that traditionalists believed to be at the expense of long-established monastic values, resulting, in their opinion, in a scanty and perhaps inadequate vocational education. To be sure, many monks and nuns found it difficult to maintain a commitment to silence and prayer, to deep contemplation, in the fray of community service.

By the mid-twentieth century, the missionary thrust among the Benedictines had abated, largely because of changes occurring in American society. Among American Catholic laity, there was a new sense of individual responsibility for the care of one's soul. Greater educational and employment opportunities, especially for women, prompted many to question the relevance of a religious vocation. Activities that had once been the province of religious organizations—hospitals, certain welfare programs, mission and parochial schools and other educational efforts—were by now taken over to a large extent by the secular society. Certainly today there are Benedictine monastic communities that continue their outreach work. Many have created the monasteries that are now found in almost every country of the world: there are some 8,400 Benedictine monks in 250 independent monasteries worldwide, with forty-five houses in the United States. Yet traditionally the Benedictines, and especially the Cistercians who broke away from them centuries ago, have focused more on the contemplative life than have the apostolic, active orders such as the Franciscans or Dominicans or Paulists. Recent studies show that the more socially active missionary communities are declining in membership, while at the same time those where contemplative values are paramount are gaining members.

A measure of these changes toward a more individualistic spirituality in the focus of Americans' religious interests can be seen in the continuing popularity of the books and journals of the 20th century's most famous monk, the Trappist from Kentucky, Thomas Merton—Father Louis of Our Lady of Gethsemani Abbey. Merton's 1949 autobiography, *Seven Story Mountain,* was a bestseller, and his many books on the contemplative life captured the imagination of a public strained by the fear and insecurity of war, stressed by the demands of the workplace and the tensions and conflicts of broken family life, and alienated from a society seemingly devoted to a soulless commercialism. Merton reports that in the ten years following World War II, his monastery of Gethsemani received two thousand applicants. (According to a former guestmaster at Christ in the Desert, one response to the September 11, 2001 attack on New York and

Washington was a tremendous increase in visitors asking to spend time at the monastery.)

For many citizens, the United States is also a society educated beyond the simple acceptance of a rigid and often superficial presentation of religion. Through Merton's writings, as well of those of his Japanese friend, Daisetz Suzuki, the Vietnamese monk Thich Nhat Hanh, and such writers as Alan Watts, Suzuki-Roshi, and the translators and interpreters of the Yogi and Zen masters, Americans have become aware of the deep inner spirituality intrinsic to Eastern religions. Many flocked to Maharishi Mahesh Yogi's courses on transcendental meditation, some took up Sufi dancing, some embraced arcane New Age rituals, some explored medieval traditions of alchemy, astrology, or the Kabbalah. In the Catholic world, a new interest in Christian mysticism developed, as can be seen in the present-day regard for such mystics as Julian of Norwich, Nicholas of Cusa, Meister Eckhart, Hildegard von Bingen, Saint John of the Cross, and others, prompting a call for spiritual renewal within the Church itself. In American monasticism this call predated the more "official" decree for renewal—*aggiornamento*—that came from Pope John XXIII and his Ecumenical Council in the 1960s. One of the outcomes of the Vatican II discussions was the directive to the monastic orders to examine their rules, customs, and style of life with the specific purpose of renewing their vitality. These influences would affect both those choosing to live a contemplative life within the cloister and those who desire a temporary association with that life in order to find the spiritual renewal and strength to meet their secular responsibilities.

The move toward "Primitive Benedictinism" or "primitive observance" in certain American monasteries, as Merton discusses in his *Contemplation in a World of Action,* was for "a simple, natural, more or less hard life in contact with nature, nourished by the Bible, the monastic fathers and the liturgy, and faithful to the ancient ideal of prayer, silence, and that 'holy leisure' (*otium sanctum*) necessary for a pure and tranquil heart in which God could be experienced, tasted, in the silence and freedom of the monk's inner peace." Mount Saviour, the founding monastery of Christ in the Desert, is one of the communities that Merton mentions as embracing this primitive observance.

At the same time that he was writing about Christian renewal and the importance of our society's growing awareness of Eastern contemplative religions and their relation to Christian beliefs, Merton was also advocating against the politics of war. Considered by many, both here and abroad, to be the patron saint of the antiwar movement, he spoke out vehemently against the war in Vietnam. In his 1967 book, *Faith and Violence,* he attacked the violence of American society, labeling the war an "overwhelming atrocity." Yet in spite of his worldly renown, Merton remained a contemplative, withdrawing to his hermitage on the grounds of the Kentucky abbey to study and write and pray. He strongly believed in the values of the monastic life: "While not blindly rejecting and negating the modern world, the monastery nevertheless maintains a certain critical distance and perspective, which are absolutely necessary as mass society becomes at once more totally organized and more mindlessly violent." As much as Merton valued his silent life in the hermitage, the celebrity of his activist writings continually brought admirers to the abbey to visit him—precisely as a monastic principle counsels: "The more you distance yourself from the world, the more the world will seek you out."

During his two visits in 1968 to Christ in the Desert—a few months before his accidental electrocution by a faulty fan in a Red Cross center in Bangkok—Merton was struck by the dedication to the contemplative life he perceived among the monks in their remote river canyon. To him, the monastery on the Chama was "a place where all may experience the peace which the world cannot give." His interest in the meditative practices of Eastern religions prompted him to consider the establishment of an East-West center that would be a forum for international peace, a place where the leaders of the world's religions could come together in dialog. One purpose for his fateful trip to the Far East had been to discuss this idea with his Buddhist friends. We find in his journals that he considered Christ in the Desert a possible venue for such a center. But with his death, his plans died with him.

Whether Merton would have chosen Christ in the Desert as the ideal place to establish his center, we cannot know. Subsequent to his death, both the Thomas Merton Foundation and the international Merton Society were established to perpetuate his ideas and to publish his many journals, photographs, and correspondence. But an East-West center has not developed as he had proposed. We do know from his journals that during his stay in the Chama Canyon, Merton was profoundly moved by the beauty of the landscape and the simple life of work and prayer that he found there, and which exemplified the Benedictine primitive observance.

To find a place appropriate for this primitive observance "in the tradition of Saint John the Baptist" was the mission that Prior Damasus gave Father Aelred when he sent him out from Mount Saviour over forty years ago to establish a new monastery.

7

A Different Desert

The final achievement of the desert: to come at last to love the whole world with an all-embracing love.

—Father Aelred Wall

*D*espite the problems Brother Ansgar wrote about in the early years of the monastery, he also states that he loved the life of the canyon, the quiet flow of the river, the sheer rock cliffs, their articulated faces stained with the varnish of ages. During the winters, when the Offices were held in the convento because the uninsulated chapel was too cold to use, Ansgar was touched that Father Aelred included the monastery cats and dogs in the celebrations. Nevertheless, Ansgar tells us, he did not have confidence in Father Aelred as a superior.

Amy Richardson, in the letter she wrote to the monks about her two-year stay working at the monastery, comments that "Father Aelred might start a project, but not have the patience to carry it out." Already in 1969 she had the feeling that Aelred "was beginning to crack." She writes: "[There were] signs of over-insistence, a distracted air in his clear blue eyes, an inability to concentrate on any one thing, and sort of a peripheral anxiety, as I think he saw the numerous threats against the monastery, its privacy, its place in the community, its very existence." In another letter she writes, "In 1972, Father Aelred was quite depressed that winter. He brooded a lot and had arguments with Andronico and Mike. It was not a cheerful community. Things were going decidedly downhill."

Father Aelred made the statement quoted above—that the desert would bring one to an all-embracing love—shortly after 1964 when he arrived in the canyon to build the monastery of his dreams. If, in 1972, he still believed this, the desert he had in mind was not the desert of the Chama Canyon. The disappointments and disasters of the last eight years—the squabbles over construction, the numerous accidents, the failure of his plan to make goat cheese or to raise sheep as a means of self-support for the monastery, the constant demands on peace and privacy involved in running a guesthouse, the insistent tension of financial insecurity, the disagreements with his brothers, and the failure of his idea of a lay community at the monastery, let alone the sometimes devastating vagaries of the weather—had all become too much for him. Ill, discouraged, exhausted, and angry, Aelred resigned that year as prior of Christ in the Desert.

Father Aelred's friend, right-hand man, and manager of the monastery farm, Andronico Gallegos, reports receiving a phone call from the priest asking him to bring his wife Ida and meet him at the Rio Grande Café in Española. After a friendly dinner, Aelred asked Andronico to take him to Santa Fe to the bus station. Aelred had said nothing to the two about leaving the monastery; merely that he wanted a ride to Santa Fe. Andronico had no idea they were sharing a last supper; he never saw his friend again.

Apparently only later Aelred wrote to the three monks at the monastery, Brothers Anthony and Francisco and Father Gregory, that he was going east to solicit funds, but would not return. Father Tarcisius, a monk from Gethsemeni who subsequently joined the brothers for a time, recalls that Aelred's relationship with Father Gregory had disintegrated to the point that the two professed monks refused to speak to each other and communicated by writing notes, delivered by their brothers. What made this situation especially bitter was that originally the two monks had been close friends. Aelred had been a student at Portsmouth Priory when Gregory was a monk there, and later they were brothers together at Mount Saviour. Perhaps Aelred's primary disappointment, however, was that he had been unable to form a stable community. The brothers had come, stayed for a while, and left. None of them had committed to remaining permanently in the rugged canyon.

Aelred traveled in the United States and Mexico, finally retiring to a hermitage that he called Nuestra Señora de la Soledad, some ten miles from the town of San Miguel de Allende. Since foreigners were not permitted to purchase land in Mexico, friends in San Miguel held the deed to a 33-acre parcel of land for him. The property had two small buildings on it that were similar to the little ranch house he had once bought from Andronico's brother, Juan Gallegos. Aelred remodeled one of the buildings into a hermitage, and the other into a guesthouse. His mother and his sister and her family soon joined him for an extended visit, as did many friends from New Mexico.

Father Aelred's first years at La Soledad were not unlike the early days at Christ in the Desert. He drew his water from the river to irrigate a garden and raised vegetables and flowers that he sold to hotels in San Miguel. He established a *taller*, or workshop, for local craftsmen, and arranged for the workers to sell their carvings in the Mexican hotels and also at the import shop, Artesanos, in Santa Fe. He enjoyed living more or less alone at La Soledad, away from the demands of monastic life, yet he hoped that someday a monastery might be built on his property.

Priscilla Bunker, who with her family was a frequent guest at La Soledad, comments that Father Aelred was genuinely happy in Mexico. She concludes that many of the problems at Christ in the Desert occurred because Aelred and the others didn't know how to carry out the dream. Both the monks and their working guests were city-bred. Andronico was the only one who knew how to work the land. Priscilla recalls that one day she found Brother Anthony scraping off the valuable topsoil from the garden. When she stopped him, he said that he thought it would be the easiest way to get rid of the weeds. When Anthony was told that he had planted the carrots much too late in the year for them to grow, his response was, "If God is on our side, they'll grow." They didn't. Apparently God didn't think much of Brother Anthony as a farmer. The difference for Father Aelred in Mexico is that he had the knowledgeable help from the villagers close to La Soledad.

George Nakashima's beautiful chapel at Christ in the Desert had been a gift to Father Aelred from his mother. When she died, Aelred asked Nakashima to design a little chapel at La Soledad in her memory. The chapel is completely different from the one on the Chama. Round-domed and white, it is reminiscent of a Greek village church and completely in harmony with the dry desert landscape of Mexico.

Father Aelred spent the rest of his life at La Soledad. He died on November 13, 1984 and is buried there. He never returned to Christ in the Desert.

George Nakashima's Chapel at La Soledad.

☙ 8

A Monk's Life

The prayer of the
monk is not perfect
until he no longer
realizes himself or
the fact that he is
praying.
—Saint Antony of
the Desert

A man who hears the call to serve God, may wish to answer that call in a number of ways—perhaps by living a spiritually cognizant life as a husband and father; perhaps by the manner in which he conducts his business affairs; perhaps by his work as a teacher, a writer, a priest, a minister. Or perhaps he may wish to withdraw completely from the secular world to devote his life to seeking God in a monastic community with others who have been called as he has.

If a man wishes to join the community at Christ in the Desert, most likely he will make several initial visits to the canyon as a guest. Perhaps he may be invited to live with the brothers for a few weeks. He may then formally ask to become a postulant, which, if he is accepted, will allow him to participate in the life of the community for about six months. At this point he will be asked to leave the monastic environment for a month to reflect on his experiences at the monastery and to consider the strength of his call. If he decides that, indeed, he does want to pursue becoming a monk, and the brothers agree, he will return to enter the novitiate for a year of study—Scripture, Saint Benedict's *Rule*, and writings on philosophy, monastic history, and doctrine. At this time he will receive a novice's habit and a new name. During this year, he will be "formed" through study and prayer under the guidance of the novice master.

There are a couple of catches up front. To apply to formally join the monastic community, he must be between the ages of twenty-five and forty, and he must be a member of the Catholic Church. And of course he must feel a genuine calling to the cenobitic life. The monastery is, in Saint Benedict's words, "a school for the Lord's service;" it is not a refuge for misfits from the greater society. Whatever problems an individual might try to escape will be doubly amplified in the intensely tight, closed society of a monastic community. As Thomas Merton wrote: "If you regard contemplation principally as a means to escape from the miseries of human life, as a withdrawal from the anguish and suffering of this struggle, you do not know what contemplation is, and you will never find God."

The age limit is simply practical. According to Brother André, experience has taught that men older than forty are used to a life of self-determination and independence, and often find it difficult to honor the vow of obedience. Not to say that younger ones may not find it difficult as well—there are departures all along the way. For this reason the monastery insists on years of study and exposure to monastic life before the individual makes a final, solemn commitment to the community.

In his book, *The Frontiers of Paradise*, a thorough and often humorous study of monks and monasticism, the English poet and former Jesuit, Peter Levi, writes, "the noviceship is a time when not so much the genuineness as the durability of a religious vocation is tested. A temporary enthusiasm may be genuine enough, but religious institutions insist on permanence and stability.... There do exist states of illusion or false vocation, though they can sometimes be diagnosed only in retrospect. One of the most frightening is the condition of some chaste young man who has an overwhelming experience of beauty and joy that he takes for the presence of God, though its real basis is simply the emergence of suppressed sexuality without an object....The chaste young man's experience is almost ecstatic. His later experience, when adolescence is over and he finds himself in his monastery, will be a cumulative and bitter sense of loss, of the absence of the God of his youth."

Assuming the novice survives—or perhaps better, transcends—the condition Levi warns of, and he wishes, and his superiors approve, he makes his preliminary, "simple" vows: obedience, stability, and conversion of life. Obedience is voluntarily and willingly given to the superior; stability means that he intends to remain at the monastery and persevere in his vocation; conversion of life includes a commitment to celibacy, but implies an even greater conversion, a *metanoia* of the self, a turning oneself "inside-out," a transformation of the self from the person he was in the outside world into a man of God.

The period of the monk's preliminary vows lasts from three to as many as nine years, during which he further determines the strength of his commitment to the contemplative life, his willingness to live by the *Rule*, and his ability to persevere in his vows. When he and his superiors determine he is ready, he makes his final, solemn vows. They are the same vows he made previously, but this time they bind him for life. Once a monk has made these final vows, to break them is to break a promise to God. In acknowledgment of his solemn vows he is given the monastic cowl to wear during certain liturgical services as a sign that he is now a permanent member of the community.

At this time, the monk must give up all his worldly possessions: money, property, personal effects, even his books, (a requirement which may account for the eclecticism of the monastery library.) As the Evangelist Luke said in the Acts of the Apostles, *All who believed were together, and had all things in common.* If the monk has any wealth, he need not give it to the monastery or to the Church if he doesn't wish to, but he is no longer permitted to hold it. Should he come into an inheritance after making his solemn vows, he is not allowed to determine its distribution.

In return, the monastery makes a commitment to him: to keep him in sickness and in health for the rest of his life. He must be supplied with such worldly necessities as food, clothing, a cell for study and sleep, money to buy personal items, money to travel when necessary, medical care, and perhaps educational opportunities. While there may be time away for longer visits to another monastery, for education, or for personal family matters, the monk always returns to his home house. He makes his vow of stability to a specific community, and only rarely will he be given permission to relocate permanently to another monastery.

This is the road an individual takes to *become* a monk. The same road is followed by the woman who wishes to become a nun, and this discussion applies to women as well as to men. As to what *is* a monk, however, it is best to let a monk speak to that. Brother Christian Leisy, currently the prior at Christ in the Desert, has written here his understanding of the monk's call to serve God from the point of view of a participant in monastic life.

What is a monk? There is no one or simple answer to the question, even though the origin of the word "monk" relates to the idea of "one" and "simple." Monks exist in the Hindu, Christian, Buddhist, and Tibetan Bön traditions among world religions. Within the Christian tradition there are Catholic, Orthodox and Protestant monks. And within the Catholic tradition, Benedictine, Cistercian, Carthusian, Jeronomite, Maronite, Adoration, and various other "orders" of monks.

As the members of the Monastery of Christ in the Desert are Benedictine monks, these thoughts focus on that type of monk, though much of what is said might apply also to other Christian monks, and perhaps to monks of other religions as well.

Benedictine monks and nuns are "seekers of God." Guided by Saint Benedict's sixth century *Rule for Monks*, they are men and women who have felt a call from God to embrace a celibate lifestyle and to live in community, subject to the authority of an abbot or abbess, who is seen as holding the place of Christ in the monastery. The monk and nun give their lives to the praise of God in public and private prayer, and to some kind of work, manual or intellectual, to help the monastery earn an income. Reading is also an important aspect of the monk's day; hence prayer, work, and reading are understood as the "three pillars" of Benedictine monastic life. This has been compared to a three-legged stool: if one of the legs is missing or out of proportion, the structure will fall.

Believing that God has revealed himself in the history of humankind, and that this revelation is recorded in the sacred texts of the Jewish and Christian traditions, the monk holds that God is "alive and well," and can be known. Communion with God is thus possible for human beings, and the monk enters into this communication at specific times and places through prayer. This occurs especially in the daily round of prayers carried out in the choir of the monastery church. The monks gather from pre-dawn until early evening to spend ten minutes to an hour or more in structured worship, chanting the Book of Psalms, a collection of 150 poems of varying lengths contained in the Hebrew Scriptures. At Christ in the Desert, the Psalms are generally sung in English—although occasionally in Latin—to the ancient melodies of Gregorian chant.

Benedictines believe the Psalms and other biblical texts of Hebrew and Greek origin that are used for community prayer are divinely inspired. Being for us the very word of God, the texts are a message of salvation, peace, and love directed to humans by an all-powerful, loving, and ultimately knowable God. In the Christian tradition, God is called by many names: Father, Lord, Creator, Holy Spirit, Good Shepherd, Redeemer, King of Glory, Daystar, Adonai, Emmanuel, Jesus Christ, Son of God, Mighty One, Heavenly Ruler, to mention just a few of his titles.

We believe God is made known to us in our communal worship, but also in the silence of our hearts when we pray in private. In that sense we never pray alone, for we believe that praying with us and in us is the company of saints and angels—what is called the "communion of saints"—united in the triune God: Father, Son, and Holy Spirit in paradise forever. A monk is expected to dedicate some hours each day to community and solitary prayer through the scriptural texts and in silence, as well as through acknowledgement of the grandeur of creation and even in daily interactions with others.

The life of prayer will vary from one individual to another, from this year to the next, so it is never easy to generalize about such an intimate part of the Benedictine experience. Binding together with like-minded people, however, assures support in the inevitable challenges to persevering in prayer, especially when it might seem useless or unfulfilling. This occasional—sometimes frequent—doubt is likely to occur for a Benedictine or for any other kind of monk, Christian or otherwise, who is dedicated to the worship of God.

A life of worship requires material support. This can be obtained through begging or by engaging in work that can produce an income to sustain monastic life. Benedictines are not traditionally mendicants or beggars, but in fact they often do have to rely on the generosity of benefactors in order to survive or supplement their income. At the same time, Benedictines are obliged to seek work compatible with their monastic existence—work that normally can be carried out within the monastery, and such that can be reasonably accomplished within the course of a day and in limited daily work periods. This work might include raising animals, making food products such as cheese, fudge, wine or beer, perhaps raising bees, writing books or making handicrafts such as photo cards, rosaries, candles, and sacred images for purchase by visitors to the monastery or its website. No one type of work is specifically "Benedictine"—other than perhaps manufacture of the traditional, famous cognac of an earlier time—but work, itself, certainly is. Besides providing a source of income, manual or intellectual work undertaken by Benedictine monks is a means of exercising motor and rational skills in the service of the monastery and of humankind in general.

Among Benedictines, the work of hospitality is especially honored. People are welcomed to spend some days or weeks at the monastery, usually lodged in a guesthouse and sharing in the prayer, work, and meals with the monks. Inherent in this work is the necessary correspondence, housekeeping, greeting the guests and organizing their stay by one or more of the monks. This provides another opportunity to put one's hands to work and give one's heart to God within the walls of the monastic enclosure.

Every monk who is able is expected to make some contribution to the upkeep and income of the monastery. Some of the work, for example, cooking, cleaning, correspondence, and maintenance, is not directly income producing, but necessary nonetheless. Other work, such as crafts or writing, is income producing. Usually the guesthouse is a source of income, as is a gift shop, often found at monasteries today. No one type of work is considered better or more important than another. The abbot, in conjunction with his cellarer and the council of deans, seeks to find suitable jobs for everyone. The aged and infirm have to be taken into account, and often are not able to contribute directly to the monastery. Of course, in some cases they can, and hence their contribution must not be overlooked. Those unable to work and who must be served are never considered "useless" or "undesirable." They, too, contribute by their prayers, by their example and perseverance, and as past providers for the monastery, now enjoying a respite.

Connected to both prayer and work is the third pillar of the Benedictine structure, namely reading. Saint Benedict, in his *Rule,* was very clear that the monks of his time should know how to read. Not everyone would have been able to read in the church or the refectory to the edification of the listeners, but all should at least know how to read to themselves, in order to absorb the teachings of sacred Scripture and the commentaries by Church saints and monastic authors.

In modern culture books abound, but the discipline, indeed the fine art of reading is often unknown nowadays to many entering monastic life. Television, the Internet, and other modern inventions can block the easy ability to pick up a book, stick with it to the end, and profit from its wisdom.

Each day Benedictine monks are occupied for some hours with sacred reading—*lectio divina,* the "holy reading" of the monastic tradition—contemplating the words of the Bible, as well as writings by ancient and modern authors in the spiritual tradition of the Church. A library is thus an important part of the monastery complex, and the monks are encouraged to find suitable books to advance their spiritual life. Time spent in *lectio divina* is considered as important for the monk as time spent in prayer and work.

How are the three activities—prayer, work, and reading— meant to interact? For a Benedictine monk there should be some time every day for each of the three pillars. It would not be suitable to spend the whole day just in prayer and not working or reading, or working all day and not reading or praying. A monastery is usually structured with specific prayer, work, and reading periods. A healthy balance of the three should be sought each day.

Inevitably the proper balance will vary from one monk to the next. Some might be content with doing nothing but praying, or working from sunrise to sunset, or curling up with a book the entire day. Usually, however, these extremes are not possible in the context of an observant monastery, where various needs and expectations exist on a daily schedule, and where one cannot follow personal preferences. There may be times in the monastery schedule for a periodic day of solitude—as in Christ in the Desert's monthly "Desert Day""—or an annual retreat, or a visit to one's family. At such times, the balance of prayer, work, and reading may of necessity be altered, but this is understood as the exception rather than the norm in the life of a monk.

Is any one of the three pillars more important than the others? This is difficult to say, but certainly prayer is at the heart of a life rooted in faith in Jesus Christ as the center of one's existence. He who prays desires to put prayer into his work and to foster that prayer with reading—above all the Scriptures, but other edifying texts as well.

Like all human beings, the monk is not a "finished product," but rather a "work in progress." The monk may reach a degree of discipline, self-mastery, or focus that he may not have been capable of five, ten, or twenty years earlier. Nonetheless, as long as he is alive, the monk is always seeking to go deeper to God, to grow in love and freedom before God, to keep on the path that leads to God.

There may be setbacks along the way; the monk may even stray completely from the right path. This is often described as "falling into sin." But the tradition of Christian monasticism is rooted in "getting up" by the grace of God and carrying on, even when one has failed in minor or major ways. For Catholics this process is greatly assisted by the sacrament of Reconciliation or Confession. When the monk seeks absolution and performs his penance, spiritual healing can take place. He may also desire to disclose the failures of his journey to a superior or a trusted guide, and seek an encouraging or challenging word in order to find direction, new courage, or correction along the way to God.

Saint Benedict is called the "Father of Western Monasticism." A shrewd judge of character, he realized the strong and the weak, the humble and the proud, the timorous and the courageous, the young and the old would populate his monastery. One of the more daunting tasks of the superior is to adapt to the various temperaments of his monks and find appropriate means of leading each one along the journey from self-centeredness to Christ-centeredness. There is no one blueprint or model that can be applied to everyone; hence a certain tension inevitably exists in a monastery. A wise abbot adjusts the means of moving his flock forward in the ways of God, both as a community and as individuals. One monk may need a one-time-only, ever so mild coaxing, another a decidedly more vigorous correction, another a repeated but gentle admonition to "get with the program," to give one's life wholly to God within the monastic community. Another may have to be told that things are simply not working out, and that some other way of life is apparently the only solution to the problem.

In Saint Benedict's time, once one entered the monastic state, perseverance and permanence were much more common than in the fluid and commitment-allergic age we live in today. Hence, extreme care must be exercised so as not to frighten off the weaker hearted. Yet there is no running from the fact that hardships and demands are inherent in the monastic way of life.

Monasticism has been part of the Christian experience since the third century, and in its Benedictine form since the sixth century. No other institution or culture in the Church has endured as long as monasticism, and monks can be justifiably proud of this fact. That doesn't diminish, though, the rigors and challenges that monasticism presents to its adherents at any time or place. For those who persevere, there is always the anticipation of true freedom in the Lord, the desire to achieve the "one thing necessary," namely God and the kingdom that Jesus Christ came to announce, and whose gates he opened so that all might enter.

Benedictine monasticism is one path among many that Catholics can take to reach their goal of life on high, where Christ is seated at God's right hand. Dante Alighieri used this image in the *Divine Comedy*, where he describes heaven as "joy past compare; gladness unutterable; imperishable life of peace and love; exhaustless riches, and unmeasured bliss."

Ordination of Brother Christian by Archbishop Sánchez, 1988.

9

Of Flying Cows, Snakes, Brujos, and Monks

*F*or many years, before it was moved to accommodate the construction of the new buildings, the monastery cemetery was around the side of the chapel. It contained three graves. Two supported wooden crosses, each heading a mounded garden of thistles and chamisa. Beneath the first mound lay the mortal remains of Tom McMahon, a friend of Father Aelred; beneath the second, those of a young rock climber who had tried to climb the orange canyon walls. Ever since the tragic death in 1976 of the climber, Peter Avery, visitors who arrive at the monastery with ropes and climbing shoes are first warned not to attempt the cliffs; then, if necessary, invited to leave. Unfortunately, in 2000, a woman climber who was not a guest climbed the cliffs above the monastery and fell to her death. Since the brothers had been unaware of her presence on the monastery property, they paid no attention to the circling vultures for several days.

The third grave was a yawning, six-foot hole. A pile of shoveled dirt, long covered with weeds, lay at its lip. According to the guestmaster, the brothers dug the grave during warm weather, in case a grave might be needed at some time when the ground was frozen. A particularly zealous novice felt called to sit at the bottom of the empty grave and contemplate the meaninglessness of earthly vanities. After spooking the brethren for several months with this morbid method of meditation, the novice finally achieved enlightenment. The message was that the cenobitic life was not for him.

The monastery lies some fifteen miles upriver from the 23,000-acre Ghost Ranch Presbyterian Conference Center, which is located a few miles north of the village of Abiquiú and shortly before the turn-off to the dirt road leading into the Chama Canyon. According to Leslie Poling-Kempes's excellent history of the area, *Valley of the Shining Stone*, local legend tells us that in the 1860s and 1870s, there was a sheep camp at the entrance to the steep, rock-walled canyon of Ghost Ranch, where the conference center headquarters are now located. The shepherds would never stay long at the camp, however, because of their fear of the voices of "ghosts quarreling with each other." Apparently, fighting in the canyon between sheepherders and cattlemen had left several of them dead, and their white ghosts could be seen scaling the canyon walls at night, uttering agonized groans. As if this wasn't unsettling enough, a deadly flying cow terrorized the inhabitants of the canyon camp, and at sundown, a giant, child-eating snake would appear.

Perhaps it was the uneasy and sometimes explosive mixture of cultures coexisting in the area—the Spanish and the Utes, Kiowas, Comanches, Navajo and Apaches, as well as the *genizaros*, the baptized Indian slaves who often as not retained beliefs from their original tribes—that accounts for the susceptibility of the local people to such wild imaginings. The Spanish had brought a well-developed lore of sorcery and witchcraft with them from their European homeland, and the indigenous groups had their own native superstitions and tales of the supernatural.

Already in the mid-1700s, charges of *maleficio*, or sorcery, flew about the settlements in and around Abiquiú. A deadly plague that swept through the area was blamed on *maleficio*; women were known to fall into a trance during Mass and scream obscenities at the priest. Poor Padre Toledo was kept busy night and day exorcizing demons. An unfortunate consequence of this is that all known signs of prehistoric Indian "paganism" in the area—petroglyphs, shrines, sacred caves—were systematically destroyed by the settlers with help from the apparently equally susceptible royal troops from Santa Fe.

According to Poling-Kempes, in 1892, two brothers from the Archuleta family built a homestead on the Rito del Yeso in the canyon of the earlier sheep camp. The steep walls surrounding the homestead proved to be an ideal place to harbor stolen cattle, as well as a good place to hide corpses. Buyers who came to purchase—or to reclaim—the rustled cattle mysteriously disappeared. They were never seen again, although later, their horses could be found among those of the Archuleta brothers. At night, the groans of the murdered spirits could be heard all along the Chama River, and the Archuleta brothers' homestead soon became known to the locals as the "Rancho de los Brujos"—the Ranch of the Witches, or Ghost Ranch—and their old homestead is now the "Ghost House" on the ranch.

Historian Marc Simmons writes in his book, *Witchcraft in the Southwest,* that for the Catholic Hispanics, Christian symbols provided the strongest protection against *brujería.* Pack animals wore protective crosses on their harnesses; crosses were placed above entries, and the doors painted the blue of the Virgin's mantel so that she, too, would protect the house from the Devil's connivances. Just as vampires are said to flee when a cross is held up to them, crosses were often waved in the face of someone suspected of being a *brujo.* Brother Francisco remembered this power of the cross one day in the 1980s when he and Sister Mary Joaquín were accosted by bandits while driving on a deserted back road in Mexico. The two feared for their lives, knowing that victims seldom survive such confrontations. Brother Francisco pulled out the wooden cross he was wearing under his shirt and waved it in the faces of their attackers. The *banditos* fled in horror.

Simmons writes that actions against individuals believed to be witches could be extreme, with the authorities often paying little attention to the crimes. In 1884, T.D. Burns reported in *The New Mexico Review* the shocking murder of a woman believed by villagers to be in league with the Devil. She was taken from her home, stripped of her clothes, and shot and stabbed many times. The report said that although the authorities knew the perpetrators, no attempt had been made to arrest them.

Witches come in both genders in northern New Mexico, and are said to inhabit the caves and twisting draws of the arroyos, the ancient Anasazi ruins, and the long-abandoned ranches that once grew along the broad river terraces of the Chama. *Brujo* sightings are rare—far rarer than in the old days—and tend to appear only when something is terribly awry in the land.

One evening in 1976, shortly before sunset, a visiting priest, Father Hugh Cleary, took a walk up the canyon beyond the monastery. Looking up at the cliffs, he noticed the dark, obscure figure of a monk perched high on a ledge, bathed in the red light of the setting sun. Father Cleary waved to the monk but got no response. Later, he asked the guestmaster to apologize for him to the brother up on the cliff ledge for perhaps disturbing the man in his evening prayers. The guestmaster laughed and said, "That was no monk. That was a *brujo.*" Father Cleary had never heard the word before, and asked the guest master to explain. "*Brujos* are evil spirits," the priest was told, "demons that roam the terrain looking for someone to devour." Father Cleary was amazed at the matter-of-fact manner in which the guestmaster imparted this information, as if demons were an everyday affair at the monastery. The priest went back up the canyon at sunset for many days thereafter looking for the *brujo*, but didn't see him again.

A few days later, Peter Avery arrived in the canyon, and he and Father Cleary struck up a conversation. Peter told the priest that he had had an argument with his wife, and that he was going to climb up on the Mesa de las Viejas to meditate and pray. He never returned.

The story of Peter Avery's demise was recounted one late December afternoon in 1992 to a group of guests gathered around the crackling wood stove in the gift shop. At that time the gift shop was located in the guesthouse, and Brother Bernard was on gift shop duty that day. There were no visitors to the shop; the weather was cold and snowy, and the road was layered with thick, muddy slush. After a while, the talk turned to *brujería,* and Brother Bernard told the group that he had a story about the monastery *brujo.*

"You've all seen the grave of the rock climber up by the chapel," he began. "Well, that grave has a mystery related to it. The incident occurred several years ago, well before my time here. Peter Avery was a friend of the monks, in fact he had been a candidate here for a while, but he had left to return to the outside world. He had married and was back in the canyon just for a visit. An accomplished rock climber, he set out with his gear to climb up the rock walls to explore the Mesa de las Viejas above the canyon. He didn't return for the evening meal, and the monks became concerned. When he didn't return for Compline, they were afraid something terrible might have happened. At daybreak the next morning, the brothers set out to look for their friend. Their party included a visiting priest, and the brothers pressed him to help with the search. They prowled the cliffs and crevices all day with no success. At daybreak the following morning, the brothers gathered in the refectory to discuss what they should do. They decided it was time to call in the state police. I'm told the visiting priest spoke up and said, 'Let's wait for the other brother.' The monks assured him everyone was present, but the visitor insisted that just a few minutes before, when he was walking to the refectory in the early dawn light, he had seen a figure wearing a monk's tunic waving to him from a ledge high on the cliff beyond the chapel. It was a place the monks had missed in their search, and they immediately went to investigate. The *brujo* had vanished, but they found the body of their friend."

When Brother Bernard finished his story, the group in the gift shop was silent. He got up and put another log in the stove. "Of course we monks don't believe in *brujos*," he turned to his listeners with a smile, "but I'm told that the community prayers during the Offices were extremely jittery for the next several days."

According to Brother Bernard, the monastery *brujo* had been very helpful to the monks. Apparently there are good *brujos* and bad *brujos*.

The *brujo* story of Peter Avery's death has become legend, and as with most legends, the story changes in the telling, the retelling and the telling again. It comes alive each time it's told because it is subject to constant variation. Brother Bernard was not a member of the monastery when the event occurred, hence his story, too, is only hearsay. The story has a very different course of events when told by the monk who was Peter's friend, Brother Edward Shivell of Mepkin Abbey, and who was present at Christ in the Desert that winter day in 1976.

According to Brother Edward, Peter Avery was a student at Saint John's College in Santa Fe and came regularly to the monastery. His wife did not always come with him—she seemed to have a premonition, a sense of foreboding about the canyon. Peter was an experienced climber and had scaled the cliffs before, but since it was late in the afternoon on the day he arrived, the monks tried to dissuade him from the climb. It was a Sunday, and the monks, as was then customary on Sundays, took their meals alone. Since Peter was a guest, he wasn't expected to eat with the monks that evening, and his absence wasn't noted until the next morning, when he did not appear for Vigils, Lauds, or Eucharist. The monks set out to search the snow-covered mesa top, from where they saw a car leaving the parking lot and assumed it must be Peter's. Brother Edward stayed on the mesa for a day of solitude.

When Edward returned to the monastery, he was told that the departing car was not Peter's, and that a rescue team from Saint John's would arrive that evening. The monks searched with the team until giving up around midnight. The next day the team found Peter's footprints; he had been running. From an animal? There were no animal tracks. From a *brujo*? No one knows. The searchers followed the tracks to where they could see blood and footprints on the cliffs below. They descended the cliffs and found Peter's body close to the river. He had been in the water, but had crawled back out. He died there on the riverbank. There were no broken bones, but he had cut his leg on the descent.

Brother Edward reports he was "drawn, almost haunted," to find out what had happened to Peter on the mesa. He climbed to the mesa and traced his friend's last walk and the running tracks. Descending the cliffs from which Peter had fallen, Edward experienced what he describes as "a preternatural phenomenon"—first a blast of wind, then a scraping sound, and lastly three stomping sounds. He scooped up blood from Peter's body that had frozen in the night and carried it back to the monastery.

Unlike most legends, this one does have an "official version"—the report of the State Police. The official story is far more like that of Brother Edward, with some differences. Peter most likely jumped, rather than fell, over the last fifty feet. He had a concussion, which probably led ultimately to his demise at the river from exposure. Edward also forgot to mention that the police airplane and helicopter surveyed the area, and that there was possibly a stranger in the area.

Perhaps it was a stranger that pursued Peter, or perhaps it was a *brujo*. If the latter, it didn't leave tracks or appear to Edward that winter day on the cliffs above the monastery, so we don't know if it wore a monk's tunic. Maybe even now in this retelling, new twists have entered the

Owl Rock

legend. Sister Benedicta, for example, is convinced the *brujo* was not a monk witch, but a *bruja*—a female witch. She can even point out the cave on the canyon wall where the *bruja* lives. Andronico Gallegos, who grew up in the canyon, insists that the Chama Canyon only has female witches.

Father Tarcisius, celebrating the funeral Mass for Peter, spoke of the *brujo* as the spirit of the canyon, a spirit that was either positive or negative, depending on the attitude of the person encountering it. In his homily, Tarcisius mentioned hearing from the villagers another *brujo* legend of the canyon: *Until the big owl-shaped rock that is perched high on a cliff above the monastery falls, the canyon won't be free of its demons.* Given the rock's location over the monastery, let us hope the monks are willing to share the canyon with its demons.

One thing is certain: no one knows what or who caused an accomplished climber to run and fall and crawl into a freezing river. Peter forever holds fast the secret of his death in his grave in the monastery cemetery.

.

☜ 10
1974 and On

One meets God in the desert, but also the devil and more of one's real self than is usual in our everyday, common experience.

—Father Edward McCorkell, OSCO

*A*fter Father Aelred left for Mexico at the close of 1972, Christ in the Desert was floundering—or perhaps one should say, still floundering. The monastery's problems were not only financial: an early spring run-off took out fifty feet of riverbank, washing away part of the Brosseaus's house and the swinging footbridge across the river. The alfalfa field was flooded, and the road was so bad that visitors were constantly stuck in the mud, requiring the brothers to rescue them. The generator, which supplied electricity to the ranch house and the monks' cells, broke down. The brothers had it repaired, but as it was being lowered back into place, it fell and broke again. After that, they did without electricity, except for a small generator for power tools and to charge the battery for the radiophone. A guest had let the rams in with the ewes before the proper time the previous fall, and the ewes were dropping too early in the spring. Many of the lambs were left orphaned, and the brothers nursed them with cows' milk from baby bottles, which gave the poor creatures dysentery.

At the beginning of 1974, there were only three monks at the monastery: Brother Christopher and Father Gregory, both of whom had come from Mount Saviour, and Father Tarcisius from the Trappist Gethsemani Abbey. Because of the serious condition of his frostbitten feet, Brother Anthony, after a stay in the hospital, had returned to Mount Saviour. Clearly the small community had to attract more members or it would not survive.

Shortly after Aelred's departure, Father Gregory was appointed prior, although he would soon return to Mount Saviour because of illness. Gregory was one of the original founders of the New York monastery with Father Damasus, and although he was very concerned for the future of Christ in the Desert, in 1964 he had not supported Damasus's idea of starting another monastery. He didn't think Mount Saviour was in a position to support a foundation, and as the years went by, he clearly didn't feel that Father Aelred was an adequate superior for the job. The tension between the two monks was almost palpable, and many, including Father Aelred's family, felt that the stress of their disagreements had forced Aelred to leave. Mount Saviour still held the loan for the land at Christ in the Desert, and the New York monks felt it was time for the Chama brothers to either bring in new recruits and become self-sufficient or abandon the endeavor.

In addition to the monastery's financial straits that fall, an immediate problem was the road, which once again had become virtually impassable during the summer rains. The brothers made another appeal for funds, but half of what they received for the road repair had to be spent on shoring up the deteriorating adobe buildings. Fortunately, Ghost Ranch agreed to grade the road for them that winter.

Rumors spread that the monastery would have to close. Several religious groups were interested in taking over the property. The Benedictine Sisters of Perpetual Adoration wanted to buy it; Father Flanagan wrote to ask if he could establish his Society of the Holy Trinity there. The Mount Saviour monk and noted writer, Brother David Steindl-Rast, chair of the Connecticut Center for Spiritual Studies, advocated building a cluster of hermitages, a "laura"—small cells for an ecumenical religious community—at the north end of the monastery property. His plan was that the hermits would also use the existing guesthouse as a place to offer spiritual retreats. Steindl-Rast, like Merton, had visited the monastery in its early years and had been impressed by the beauty and remoteness of the canyon. However, his proposal was not for the kind of center that Merton had envisioned. Rather, it was for a guided retreat that would be open to lay people seeking to spend time in spiritual contemplation, away from their busy lives. The hermits would manage the retreat center, and the monastery brothers would remain on the property, but have no role in the project. This would mean that the monks would lose the use of the guesthouse for their own friends. Despite Steindl-Rast's insistence that his plan was the

A Car Stuck in the Mud: the Perennial Problem.

only way to save the monastery, the little community was convinced that Steindl-Rast and his hermits would completely take over the place; furthermore, Santa Fe's Archbishop Sánchez was decidedly against the proposal. Indeed, a retreat center would provide a means to keep the monastery alive, but the comings and goings in the canyon would destroy the contemplative nature, the "primitive observance" that was the foundation of the monastery—precisely the quality that made it so attractive to monks seeking the canyon serenity.

During 1974, Brother Edward Shivell came from the Trappist Mepkin Abbey in South Carolina to help out, and the next year Brothers Nicholas, Robert and Michael joined the community for a while. After Father Gregory returned to Mount Savior, Father Tarcisius was appointed prior, and a young monk from Mount Angel Abbey in Oregon, Brother Philip Lawrence, joined the little group to become the choirmaster and liturgist and to play the guitar for the Mass. Initially, Brother Philip had not planned to remain long; in this he was mistaken.

Georgia O'Keeffe helped the brothers with a $5,000 Christmas present that year, and with the arrival of more brothers, the monks denied talk of a closing: "We continue as a foundation of Mount Saviour under the authority of the Benedictine Abbot Primate, Dom Rembert Weakland," Prior Gregory announced most officiously in the newsletter, shortly before he returned to the Elmira monastery.

Some years earlier, in 1969, Sister Julianne Allen, a member of the International Congregation of the Sisters of Saint Mary of Namur had visited the monastery. It was a prophetic visit, an association with the monks of Christ in the Desert that would last until the present. Julianne had met Father Gregory on retreat at Mount Saviour, and had come to New Mexico to see her friend, who, at that time, was guestmaster.

To give the monks some respite from the great number of guests who wanted to visit the monastery, in 1971 Father Aelred had decided that the guesthouse would be open only in the summer. He asked Sister Julianne and two sisters from her Fort Worth community to help Priscilla Bunker and Amy Richardson oversee the guesthouse and cook for the summer guests. During these years, the guests ate with the brothers in the convento only on Saturday nights, where they shared the *lectio* and discussed the next day's Gospel and readings.

With the resignation of Father Aelred, however, his experiment of a lay community within the monastery compound was finished. Amy and Michael Richardson and their little son, Lief, had already left, and the Bunker family followed in 1975. The Lang family continued to come for long visits, but there was no longer talk of settling there. On the one hand, the departure of the two families meant that the monks no longer had their help; on the other, they had more peace and silence, and their lives back to normal as a true monastic community. The distracting presence of the families, as well as the need to maintain the guesthouse, was indicative of the conflict between the brothers' desire for a contemplative life of silence, and the need for income and practical help with the chores of the monastery.

There is no question that guests can be a problem, especially if they aren't prepared for primitive conditions. Friedl Lang tells of one woman he heard screaming for help. He rushed to find her standing on the desk in her room, pointing to a harmless bull snake that was sticking its nose in the door. Another guest complained one morning that she had searched all over the night before, but couldn't find the light switch. It hadn't occurred to her that there wasn't a light switch.

Indeed the guests can be a problem if they transgress the boundaries, both personal and territorial, the monks set to distance themselves. Yet they are a very necessary problem, for still today the guesthouse and gift shop provide the main support for the monastery.

Nevertheless, by 1974, the brothers realized that for financial reasons they had to open the guesthouse to almost year-round occupancy. Again they asked Sister Julianne and her two sisters from Fort Worth to come and oversee it for the summer.

Since the dream of cheese-making had been a failure and the sheep-raising impractical, the monks decided that they would earn their living from crafts: weaving of clerical stoles and other vestments, as well as icon and retablo painting, pottery, and woodworking projects that could be sold in the monastery gift shop and by mail order.

Two local artists, Nancy and Janusz Kozikowski from the village of Medanales, taught the monks to weave, and for the next several years, weaving and other crafts were an important source of income. The monks tried an ecumenical experiment in monastic living for a week at the guesthouse jointly with Ghost Ranch Presbyterian Center. This brought them a week's worth of visitors' donations. Such endeavors, as well as the crafts, farm produce, and the guesthouse comprised their income.

In addition to the tenuous financial situation, in 1974 the brothers were experiencing what might be termed an identity crisis. Although the monastery was a Benedictine foundation, for a time there were as many Trappist monks in the Chama Canyon as there were Benedictines. A Trappist had been involved with the community from the beginning when the monk, Father Denis Hines, had come to build the tiny stone hermitage along the river north of the main compound. Thomas Merton, also a Trappist, had considered returning to the Chama to live as a hermit. The newly appointed prior, Father Tarcisius, was a Trappist, as was Brother Edward from Mepkin. The year before, Prior Gregory had sent a letter to various Trappist monasteries in the United States inviting them to send some of their brothers to help Christ in the Desert, since the remote monastery was ideal for monks seeking a simple, contemplative life that was a living expression of Saint Benedict's *Rule*. Father Tarcisius and Brother Edward had answered that call, and later in 1976, another Trappist, Brother John Crocker, came for a time.

Indeed, the simple life at Christ in the Desert was similar to that of the Trappist tradition. Father Tarcisius pointed out in a letter to Mount Saviour that Father Damasus had based much of the life at the Elmira monastery on Trappist observances, and that this was true to an even greater extent at Christ in the Desert. Brother Edward recalls that, "for the most part the liturgy conformed to that of Gethsemani. "

Trappists are monks of the Cistercian Order. Abbot Edward McCorkell, a Cistercian from Berryville, Virginia, visited Christ in the Desert in 1974 and wrote that, for him, the monastery offered "…an authentic Cistercian experience. With no electricity one has a much more real awareness of the contrast between light and darkness, so important in biblical and monastic spirituality." In the 11th century, the Cistercian founders at Cîteaux, and later Saint Bernard at Clairvaux, had broken away from what they felt was the spiritual laxness and decadence of many of the Benedictine monasteries, particularly the powerful and controlling Abbey of Cluny, in order to return to the simple life of Saint Benedict's *Rule*. Just so in the 20th century, the monks of Christ in the Desert were striving to live an authentic spirituality as had those early Cistercians. Father McCorkell urged his Cistercian and Trappist brothers "to give their support, in one way or another, to this monastery."

Brother Edward recalls fond memories of his time at Christ in the Desert. He remembers especially the retreats each community member made on his own. On one of his retreats, he spent a week in Gallina Canyon exploring the ruins and towers of the prehistoric Gallina Culture. "It took on the aspect of a vision quest," he recalls. Another time, Edward writes that he and one of the guests explored the Anasazi ruins on the Mesa Golondrina across from the monastery. He remembers seeing an optical phenomenon, a full-circled rainbow with reflected figures of himself and the guest in the center. (In earlier times, before modern science identified the atmospheric condition that causes the reflection, such an image was thought to be a demonic specter, known in Germany as the "specter of the Brocken.")

In these years the brothers created rituals of worship for special liturgical celebrations. Edward relates that on Good Friday the community processed up to the Stations of the Cross on the hill behind the chapel, taking turns carrying a large cross. The procession stopped to pray at each station. At the twelfth station, the monks nailed the Corpus to the station cross. Edward still remembers the sound of the hammer resounding in the canyon. On Easter Monday, after reading the Gospel story of the disciples on the road to Emmaus, the brothers left the chapel and walked in groups speaking of "what we have heard." At Thanksgiving, the community met in the patio of the guesthouse in front of the statue of Saint Francis. A sand painting had been prepared, with bowls at each corner that contained earth, air (feathers), water, and fire (candles).

The monks sang the canticle of the sun, then moved on to the community garden in the lower field. Sitting within a circle formed by pine boughs, the brothers listened to the celebrant read from Scripture, after which he tossed grain into the air in thanksgiving. The group then moved on to the river near the pump house and the ritual was repeated, this time tossing water from the river into the air. At the windmill, they ended their celebration by giving thanks to God for his life-giving gifts of fire, earth, water and air.

During the summer of 1975, the brothers were occasionally invited to Georgia O'Keeffe's home in Abiquiú, an historic adobe built in the mid-19th century by General José María Cháves. And they attended concerts at Ghost Ranch that O'Keeffe organized for the local people. They made a trip together to Mesa Verde, and regularly went to Santa Fe for dinner, once spending the night in a motel—much to the chagrin of the motel owner who discovered too late he had rented a single room to seven men with sleeping bags. Edward recalls getting the tractor stuck in the middle of the river. The water was extremely low that winter, and one could cross on foot by stepping on stones in the riverbed. He decided it was unnecessary to take the tractor five miles downriver to the crossing at Scull Bridge, but instead drove it into the water, where, alas, it broke down. He left it sitting in the mud, intending to deal with the problem the next day. On awakening in the morning, all he could see of the tractor were a few inches of the top. Water had been released from El Vado Dam; he had never seen the river so high. Juan Gallegos, who lived across the river at what is now the Sebastian ranch, was willing to pull the tractor out with a winch, but it was up to Edward to swim into the freezing water to do the hookup.

Because of the unusual situation of a Benedictine foundation with a Trappist prior, and with monks of both Orders present, Prior Tarcisius proposed the monastery be canonically established as an autonomous Benedictine-Trappist community under a special *Ordo Monasticus* that would allow Rome to recognize sponsorship by both Orders, and would put Christ in the Desert directly under the Benedictine Abbot Primate in Rome. The Abbot Primate, Rembert Weakland, and the Trappist Abbot General, Ambrose Southey, thought the idea of combining the two traditions unrealistic, but were willing to consider it, and counseled to "wait and see." The brothers also discussed becoming an independent diocesan monastery under Archbishop Sánchez, but that would perhaps have entailed being called to participate in diocesan work. The monks insisted on their life as contemplatives without external apostolates.

Much earlier, Father Damasus, prior of Mount Saviour, had obtained the necessary indult to establish a novitiate at Christ in the Desert. However, to become a permanent member of the Chama community, a monk would have to transfer his vows to the Elmira monastery. Mount Saviour would expect him to live in the New York monastery for three years before accepting his profession. The Benedictine Abbot Primate suggested that he could perhaps appoint a Cistercian abbot as his vicar, and all solemnly professed monks would commit to Christ in the Desert for five years as the monastery attempted to become autonomous. All discussion of a joint venture came to an end, however, when the superiors finally decided they were against the proposal.

Prior Tarcisius wanted to stay at Christ in the Desert, but since the monastery was to remain a Benedictine foundation and was not autonomous, he could not transfer his vows. Both Tarcisius and Brother Edward, who also wanted to stay if a joint relationship could be reached, felt that without the possibility of transferring their vows, they had to leave. Tarcisius moved on to study at the Theological Union in Berkeley, and Edward returned to his South Carolina monastery. Edward writes that for him, "the impact of life in the canyon—the harsh, elemental landscape and the primitive community life at the monastery—was profound."

In 1976, Brother Philip was appointed to take Tarcisius's place as prior, and the next year he transferred his vows from Mount Angel Abbey to Mount Saviour. Mount Saviour's Prior Martin was willing to waive the requirement that Philip spend three years at the Elmira monastery because there was no one else eligible for the position of prior at Christ in the Desert. (Philip later quipped, "When I became prior, it wasn't due to my great virtue—I was the only one with vows.") In 1977, Philip was ordained to the priesthood in the monastery chapel by Archbishop Sanchez. He continued as prior until 1996, when Christ in the Desert was elevated to the status of abbey, and he was elected by his brothers as the monastery's first abbot.

By 1977, there were no more Trappist brothers at Christ in the Desert, although over the years many have come for short periods of retreat.

Prior Tarcisius 1974.

11

Liturgy of the Hours

Seven times a day I have praised you. At midnight I arose to give you praise.

—Psalm 118

*I*n accordance with the ancient psalmist's call to praise, Saint Benedict presents in his *Rule* the Liturgy of the Hours. The Liturgy is the *Opus Dei*—the work of God—in which the Psalms are chanted or recited in the monastery for the seven daytime Offices and the Night Office. The saint does allow for some flexibility on rising for the Night Office, and the brothers at Christ in the Desert have stretched rising at midnight to rising just in time to be at the chapel for Vigils by four.

The Night Office—the vigil in the dark—is a prayer for the coming of light, of release from darkness. The Office opens with the petition from Psalm 50: *O Lord, open my lips and my mouth shall proclaim your praise.* Saint Benedict prescribes which Psalms should follow, the hymns to be sung, the number of readings from the Old and New Testaments, and scriptural exegeses from the writings of the Church Fathers. The routine varies slightly between summer and winter and on Sundays and solemn festivals, but Vigils always opens with the same petition. The Night Office ends, as do all the Hours, with the litany *Lord have mercy*, prayers for absent brothers and sisters, and prayers for the faithful departed.

Lauds is praise for the approaching dawn, the triumph of light over darkness, the resurrection of our lives in the resurrection of the sun. The Office opens, as do all the day Hours, with the line from Psalm 69: *O God, come to my assistance; Lord, make haste to help me.* Today, Lauds is followed by the celebration of the Eucharist, which was not scheduled in the *Rule* of 1500 years ago. For Lauds, as well as for the Eucharist, the brothers wear white cowls over their customary black habits. Benedict advises that the superior recite the Lord's Prayer for all to hear at the close of both Lauds and Vespers, "because thorns of contention may spring up," and the pledge to *forgive others their trespasses* will allow the brothers to "cleanse themselves from this kind of vice."

Benedict prescribes the Psalms for the remaining Hours—Prime, Terce, Sext, None, Vespers and Compline. Each day of the week has different Psalms for these Hours, and Vespers includes the Canticle of Mary, *Magnificat anima mea Dominum.* At Compline—the completion of the day—the brothers pray to be kept safe through the darkness. *I will lie down and sleep comes at once/ For you alone, Lord, make me dwell in safety.* Always the same Psalms (4, 90, 133) are sung, and the monk asks the Lord to *Guard me in the shadow of your wings.* This is one responsorial among several that are intoned on each of the days. After the litany, *Lord Have Mercy* and the singing of the antiphon to Mary, the abbot blesses his brothers and guests with holy water, and all leave the chapel in the silence they will keep through the night.

Saint Benedict charges, "monks who in a week's time say less than the full Psalter with the customary canticles betray extreme indolence and lack of devotion in their service." Early in the history of Christ in the Desert, the brothers—probably not out of extreme indolence and lack of devotion, but more likely out of extreme exhaustion from pouring cement, feeding the goats, repairing the road, canning the garden produce, baling the hay and alfalfa, and haranguing with contractors—only managed to go through the whole Psalter in two weeks rather than one, and they didn't celebrate Terce and None. Not until 1978 did the brothers decide to follow the *Rule* as closely as possible and chant all 150 Psalms over the seven days, beginning the cycle again at Sunday Vigils. The decision to more precisely follow the *Rule* also meant that the brothers would have to live up to Saint Benedict's injunction to forego eating the meat of four-legged animals. Conveniently, all the monastery's frozen sheep had already been consumed.

Today, a few exceptions are made in carrying out the *Opus Dei.* Not only do the brothers not rise at midnight to celebrate the Night Office, occasionally a monk is allowed to sleep past Vigils, especially if he has returned late to the monastery from some errand the night before. If the following day is a "Desert Day," no one climbs out until Lauds. Also, the brothers no longer celebrate Prime; the Psalms for that Office are incorporated into the three "Little Hours," of Terce, Sext, and None.

Since the beginning of Christianity, the Psalms have been the central prayers of the Church's communal worship. The 150 Psalms cover the entire spectrum of human emotions, from ecstatic praise and rejoicing in the bounty of God's goodness, as in Psalm 4: *You have put into my heart a greater joy/ than they have from abundance of corn and new wine*—to begging forgiveness for one's transgressions, as in Psalm 50: *Have mercy on me, God, in your kindness. / In your compassion blot out my offense*—to vengeful entreaties to God to destroy one's enemies, as in Psalm 136: *Happy the man who shall seize and smash / your little ones against the rock!*

Visitors to Christ in the Desert often question why the brothers maintain this ancient practice of chanting words that in some cases are swords of hatred and vengeance. To pray for the destruction of one's enemies seems exceedingly "un-Christian," and during the period that Father Gregory was prior, he censored these violent Psalms, and the monks and their friends did not recite them during the Divine Office.

The Gospels admonish us to love our neighbors as we do ourselves, to turn the other cheek to our enemies, to worry about the plank in our own eye, rather than the splinter in another's. Some argue that dashing children against a rock or breaking the teeth of the wicked are meant as metaphors for smashing and breaking the evil in oneself. Great poetry reveals its truths on many levels, and certainly these Psalms can be read as metaphor. But the psalmist means what he says, for the underlying message of the Psalms is a cry for justice. Indeed, as we read in *Ecclesiastes*, there is a time for every matter under heaven, a time to praise, a time to hate, and a time to kill. And the bard of these epic imprecations is speaking as a member of a nation that had suffered banishment, war, genocide, and the sacking and destruction of that which the people held most sacred. The cry for justice is a cry to God to set the world right again, and for God to do this, the evil of the world must be destroyed. It is not a nice idea; many of the Psalms are not at all "nice." But the anguish expressed and the retribution demanded is all too human. And in acknowledging the poet's humanity we must of necessity honor his suffering and despair, his hopefulness, his anger, his sorrow, his beseeching. In singing of these things, we sing of ourselves. In this country, many of us have not suffered the personal and communal violence that the poet speaks of, but the suffering and injustice are still out there in the world and must be recognized. It is in this sense that the *Opus Dei* is the monk's prayer for healing the world.

The ritual that is celebrated today at the monastery has evolved over the years since Father Aelred's time. Christ in the Desert first celebrated the Mass in English on the first Sunday of Advent in 1964. Mount Saviour was a leader in adapting the Latin words of the Offices to the vernacular. Father Basil, one of the Chama founders with Father Aelred, and Father Gregory had worked on the new translation at Mount Saviour and later at Christ in the Desert. The next year the monks began to use English for the Offices regularly. The Psalms were recited, and antiphons from the Gelineau Psalter were sung in between the recitations. At that time there were only twenty-four Psalms and their antiphons that were set to music. There was no instrumental music except when Amy Richardson played the recorder for the Mass.

In 1974, when Brother Philip came from Mount Angel, music became much more important in the monastery liturgy. Philip was the choirmaster and liturgist, and played the guitar in the chapel. He introduced the custom of singing the blessing at the main meal. Later, in 1980, when the artist, Bob Lenz, who had previously been a postulant at the monastery, gave the brothers the paintings of Saint Benedict and Saint John the Baptist, Philip introduced the mealtime songs to the two saints.

Prior to his arrival, hymns in the chapel were sung only for the entrance processional and the recessional, but soon Philip began to compose some of the responsorial Psalms. At first the music was in simple versicles, accompanied by guitar. These were just short pieces and responses. Later, Brother Christian and an oblate, Martin Jenni, joined Philip, and the three worked out the Psalms to Gregorian chant, using the Grail translation from the Hebrew for the English.

The early Church developed chanting in many regional traditions: Byzantine, Old Roman, Gallican or Frankish, Mozarabic in Spain, Ambrosian in Milan. In the late 6th century, Pope Gregory approved a codification of the Gallican-Roman tradition, hence the name "Gregorian chant." The Gallican Gregorian chant supplanted all the other forms of Western chant except for the Ambrosian, which is still today sung in Milan. We know that the early Church inherited the tradition of chanting through its Jewish roots, and that Saint Benedict writes in his *Rule* of singing the Psalms. Probably the Psalms were chanted in unison on a single tone with a note for each syllable of text. Most of the chants of the psalmody in the Gregorian tradition were written between the 5th and the 8th centuries. No names of composers are associated with them; the praise was for God, not for the individual. The chant is normally unaccompanied, the line of text sung in a simple monotone with a variation at the end. This is the style in which the brothers at the monastery chant the Psalms for the Offices.

From the 9th to the 11th centuries, the modal scales were developed, and the existing chants were accommodated to the modal scales. The simple form of singing a note for each syllable of text evolved later into a much more fluid "melismatic" form in which many notes are sung on a single syllable. At Christ in the Desert, we hear these "melismas" in the short antiphons that precede and succeed the more monotonic chanting of the Psalms themselves, and in the music sung during the Mass. While the spoken sections of the Mass are simply intoned, the sections that are sung —the *Kyrie, Gloria, Credo, Sanctus, Agnus Dei*—are extremely melismatic. The *Alleluia,* for example may stretch the "A" of the first syllable or the "lu" of the third syllable through a series of up and down movements for several measures, in a sense creating the impression of a jubilant song without words.

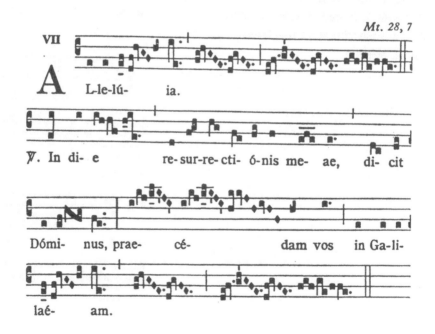

Gospel Acclamation: Melismatic Chant.

For centuries, the singers learned the music by memory, without the aid of written notation. Later a system of signs was developed—dots, checks, and short strokes—that generally indicated direction, interval, and length of tone. These signs were a configuration of hand movements for the director to use to conduct a choir that was already familiar with the chant. Finally at the end of the 10th century, a Camaldolese monk, Guido d'Arezzo, developed the four-line notation system of squared "neumes" that today is still used for writing modal music.

The tones of the traditional Gregorian chants seldom extended more than a note or two above or below the modal octave. At the height of the development of modal music in the 12th century, however, the compositions of the century's most famous nun, Hildegard von Bingen, move within a range of two and a half octaves, and her notes jump intervals that were not customary at the time. Perhaps it was the lack of formal musical education that permitted Hildegard the freedom to go beyond the established tradition and create such singularly original music as the expression of her joyous relationship to God.

With the introduction of polyphonic music into the churches and cathedrals, the Gregorian modal music lost much of its influence in the Church and was confined largely to the monasteries, which in the ensuing centuries fell on hard times. From the 12th through the 14th centuries, the gradual transformation of a rural, feudal society to an urban culture devastated the feudal economic base of the monasteries, and the massive famines and frequent attacks of bubonic plague, as well as the Hundred Years' War, severely diminished the population. Vocations declined precipitously, and many of the houses didn't survive. The number of Benedictine monks fell from 37,000 in the 14th century to a little over 15,000 in the 15th. This century also saw the rise of monastic congregations in Germany, Spain, and Italy. These provided mutual support by grouping many monasteries together. The Cassinese Congregation was one such group, the predecessor of the Subiaco Congregation to which Christ in the Desert belongs.

The Reformation had a disastrous effect on the monasteries of northern Europe, reducing the population of Benedictine monks to only 5000. Particularly in England, the monasteries were completely suppressed and the buildings largely destroyed or left to disintegrate. And what the Reformation did not accomplish, the French Revolution and its aftermath of secular scourges tried to finish.

In the mid-19th century, along with the revival of monasticism, a movement was begun to resurrect the ancient music of the Gregorian chant. The principle proponents of this movement were the monks of the Abbey of Saint Pierre de Solesmes in northern France. The Solesmes monks traveled to libraries all over Europe to copy manuscripts, comparing them and searching for agreements in the various versions until they could put together a piece of music in a uniform notation that was corrected for regional variations and scribal errors. The work the Solesmes monks produced is now universally used wherever Gregorian chant is sung.

In the 20th century, the French Jesuit, Joseph Gelineau, reworked the Jerusalem Bible Psalter in the vernacular. His original compositions were set to the "sprung rhythm" of the Hebrew Psalter, recapturing the original Hebrew poetic structure and images.

Today, there are many organizations whose mission is to publish and perform Gregorian music. Perhaps the most important of these is the Gregorian Association of London that was founded in 1870, and whose president is the Archbishop of Canterbury.

Abbot Philip once commented—paraphrasing Saint Augustine—"a prayer that is sung is prayed twice." And indeed a prayer that is sung is also remembered far better than one that is spoken, both by those who hear it and especially by those who sing it. It is the music itself, more than the words, which opens the mind to prayer. Just as in the Hindu religion, breathing the mantra empties the mind in order to open it, in the Christian West, modal chant empties the mind to center it and allow it to open to God. The resonance of the simple monochromatic lines takes over consciousness and alters perception at a deep level. Peter Levi describes the chanting of music as making "the whole of life an extended musical drama…one in which the monks take part with their entire lives." And when the music is sung in community, as it almost invariably is, there is the opening to each other in the commonality of the prayer. The Church *is* community, and as that community sings the *Hours* across the world, one is drawn closer into the communal body of Christ.

The liturgical reforms initiated by the Second Vatican Council—*aggiornamento*, or bringing the Church "up to date"—resulted in a movement away from the ritual Latin in the Mass and hence away from the Gregorian chant as well. The monks at Christ in the Desert, however, are concerned to keep the traditional Gregorian music alive. At the monastery, the Psalms are generally sung in English, but several years ago the monks reintroduced Latin in some of the music of the Mass, and four nights a week Compline is sung in Latin. The monks have also reintroduced Pope Gregory's *schola cantorum*, a solo group of singers that performs extremely melismatic chant during the Mass.

In the last few years there has been a popular revival of Gregorian chant in the secular culture. The mystical songs of Hildegard von Bingen have been rediscovered and their inherent musical qualities recognized. An early recording of Gregorian chant by the Spanish monks of Santo Domingo de Silos was reissued in 1993 and sold millions of copies, prompting groups, including the brothers of Christ in the Desert, to make recordings of their music. Because of its soothing qualities, the music is now sometimes being used in doctors' and therapists' offices. Such uses are far from the prayerful meaning of the music. It is not likely that one can concentrate on opening one's heart to God when sitting in the dentist chair—but then a monk might disagree.

In the monastic life of Christ in the Desert, the continuous daily repetition of the liturgy alters the sense of time. Time is no longer pressing forward, as in the "outside" world, in a progression of hours, days, years toward some perceived goal. Monastic time is cyclical, as the seasons of nature in the canyon are cyclical. The past is drawn into the present in living the ancient precepts of the *Rule*, in the repetition of the Psalms, in the chanting of music from centuries past, in the profound consciousness of the geologic history written on the surrounding canyon walls, the presence of ancient human habitation in the arroyos and on the mesa tops. Cyclical time is forever *Now*, and the song of the liturgy is the song of eternity in the Now.

This perception of time frees the monastic from concern over what he or she must do tomorrow, and allows one a timeless openness to enter into a deep spirituality. The commitment to living simply removes the sense of striving for gain, so insistent in the outside world. Of course a monk can't completely escape the *kronos* of that world—an appointment with the dentist, a trip to the supermarket, time away for schooling or attendance at a conference, a necessary trip to Española for a free haircut from Don Carlos—but one can return from that world into an altered dimension of time.

There is a restlessness to modern life, a relentless striving to accomplish or gain something in the external world, only to find there is yet something further that must be accomplished or gained. The monk is restless too, and yet his restlessness is for something internal, an inner searching that is not time-bound. The monk seeks to allay that restlessness in chanting the sacred song of the Scriptures, and—through no contrivance of the human will—in the hourly, daily, yearly opening of his heart to the knowledge of God.

As Saint Augustine said, "Our hearts are restless until they rest in God."

12
1977 and On

They sow fields and plant their vines; these yield crops for the harvest. He blesses them; they grow in numbers. He does not let their herds decrease.

—Psalm 107

$\mathcal{T}$here were only three monks at Christ in the Desert at the beginning of 1977—Brothers Robert and Michael, and Brother Philip as prior. But over the next few years more were to come—Brothers Xavier, Thomas, Jeremy, André, Francisco, Aelred Squire, Kevin, and Cassian. Some would stay, some would leave. After a preliminary visit in 1974, Brother Christian Leisy decided against joining the little group on the Chama. Because of the confusion over whether the monastery was Trappist or Benedictine or both, he felt the community lacked focus and cohesiveness. Now that all the Trappist monks had left, however, Brother Christian changed his mind and joined the community in May, 1977.

No sooner had he arrived, than the monastery was faced with potential disaster. Ed and Roberta Brosseau of Santa Fe owned the meadowland directly across the river from the monastery. During the 1950s, the Brosseaus managed a small guest ranch. Their brochure announced the property as the "Gallina Bench Ranch, Land of the Torreones." Just getting to the ranch in 1950 must have been part of the wilderness experience. One day the Brosseaus arrived in the canyon to discover their ranch house had been destroyed by vandals. What was left of it, the river later carried away.

The couple was so discouraged they seldom came again to the property, so it was no surprise that sooner or later their land would be put up for sale. The monks had nightmares of a vacation resort or a warren of summer condos staring them in the face. That would be the end of peace in the canyon, and most probably the end of the monastery itself.

Everyone was agreed that the price for the 160 acres was fair. The problem was where to find the necessary $200,000. The Forest Service didn't have the money to buy the land, and even if it did, the land would be for recreational use, which could be a problem for the monastery. Mount Saviour couldn't come up with that kind of money either. To make matters worse, the Forest Service was in the process of establishing the east side of the Chama Canyon, beyond the edge of the road, as a Wilderness Area. While this designation was welcomed by the monks, it would also make the two remaining pieces of private land at the end of the road—the Brosseau ranch and a piece still owned by Juan Gallegos along Gallina Creek—that much more valuable, since these were the only private properties in the canyon that could be developed.

The monks had only a sixty-day deadline by which they would have to purchase the land or it would be put on the market. Contacting their friends everywhere, the monks desperately tried to raise the $200,000. At the last minute, the brothers received several large donations and again help from Santa Fe friends. In March 1978, they purchased the Brosseau property. The Gallegos property was sold shortly after to Fred and Elizabeth Berry, but given its location out of sight of the monastery, and the fact that the Berrys intended to use the land for farming (as well as the fact that the monastery owned the locked-gate easement that gave access to the farm) the brothers were finally able to sleep again at night. The community was overwhelmed at the generosity of their friends. Their gifts had saved the monastery, as well as greatly increasing its land area, which is now completely surrounded by national forest and wilderness area.

By the late 1970s, the monastery was self-sufficient. They restored the old *acequias* from an earlier time, and Brother Michael and Brother Francisco tended the vegetable garden. There were fresh eggs from the chicken coop, and the monks had plenty of produce to eat and they canned the rest. In 1978 they canned 850 quarts of beans, squash, peas, and apples, and in the mid-eighties, as many as 5000 quarts, storing the canned goods in an old generator pit and a broken cistern.

Brother Kevin at the Potter's Wheel.

A solarium, built with the assistance of the New Mexico Solar Energy Association, helped heat the convento. To save further on fuel costs, the monks began to investigate the use of solar energy in place of the kerosene lamps and propane lights. They replaced the propane heaters in all the buildings, including the chapel, with wood stoves. Their cost-consciousness went so far that when the monastery needed a new chain saw, Brother Francisco and Brother Xavier tried to win one by entering a chain saw carving competition at Chief Mike's Chain Saw Repair in Santa Fe. Alas, neither finished his masterpiece in time, and the monastery had to make do with the old saw.

The house the Bunker family had built was converted into a weaving studio, and the monks spun wool and made their own dyes from native plants of the canyon. Earlier in the 1970s, one of the brothers made the lectern that was used for many years in the chapel. With a little help from God, he fashioned a swirling piece of deadwood into the Pascal candleholder that is still used for the Easter season. Several of the brothers, including Brother Jeremy, learned to weave at the monastery. Although Jeremy left monastic life, he has continued with his art, and his weavings are now shown in galleries in Santa Fe and Taos.

With the income from the guesthouse and the weaving, pottery, and other crafts, the monastery tried to no longer depend on outside financial help. In a wildly optimistic move, the brothers even told their friends in Española they should stop fundraising for them—at least for a while.

A happy consequence of the fundraising effort that had successfully gained the monks the money to buy the Brosseau property was the reconciliation with Father Aelred. Except for Brother Christopher, who had known Aelred at Mount Saviour before he came to New Mexico, by 1977, none of the monks present at Christ in the Desert had known the founder. One of the fundraising letters was inadvertently sent to Aelred's sister, Barbara, who responded angrily to the request, charging the monks with having forgotten her brother and their family. She was further incensed that they should ask her for money, when her family had contributed so much to the initial building of the monastery. Prior Philip wrote her immediately, telling her that her name had simply been on the monastery mailing list, and that he was not aware the letter had been sent to her. He acknowledged the Wall family's significant contribution to the monastery and told her that although he was aware of the previous monks' differences with Father Aelred, he and his brothers were eager to repair the relationship with their founder. Philip went to Mexico to see Aelred at La Soledad to make peace with him. In this, Philip was successful.

Brother Jeremy Removing a Rug from his Loom.

Father Aelred was still officially a monk in vows to Portsmouth Abbey (Portsmouth Priory had become an abbey in 1969.) He told Philip he would like to transfer his vows to Christ in the Desert, but since the monastery was still a dependency of Mount Saviour, he would transfer his vows there. In this way he could be reunited with his Chama brothers from afar. Aelred's desire to become a professed member of the community, along with the new financial stability of the monastery, spurred the brothers to seek independence from Mount Saviour.

The brothers investigated several possibilities: one would be to form a new congregation with Mount Saviour and another contemplative Benedictine monastery. This would have allowed them the autonomy they needed, but it was decided that such a congregation would be too small. Another possibility was to join an existing congregation. The brothers investigated the Olivetan, the Solesmes, the Swiss-American, and the Subiaco Congregations. The first three were not interested in taking on the monastery, but in 1981, Prior Philip visited the headquarters of the Subiaco Congregation in Rome. He was directed to talk to the Visitor of the English Province of the congregation, Abbot David Parry, at Ramsgate Abbey in Kent. Abbot David visited Christ in the Desert in 1982 to determine if the monastery should be accepted. He reported favorably to the abbot president of the Subiaco Congregation, Abbot Denis Huerre. The brothers voted to join the congregation, and late in 1983, Philip became the prior of an independent house within the English Province of the Subiaco Congregation.

Since now Christ in the Desert was finally autonomous, Father Aelred would be able to transfer his vows from Portsmouth Abbey directly to the desert monastery. Although he knew he was dying, he hoped at last to belong officially to the community he had established so long ago.

Aelred never returned to the Chama Canyon. He once got as for north as Santa Fe, but turned back, unable to face his monastery again. In 1984, he succeeded in transferring his vows to Christ in the Desert, less than a year before he died in Mexico.

In 1979, Aelred had told Philip that he wished to leave his property at Nuestra Señora de la Soledad to Christ in the Desert after his death. There were thirty-three acres, of which half were tillable. There was already a woodworking *taller*, and the villagers were making furniture and wooden items for sale. There were no debts on the property, and in a year Aelred expected to become an *inmigrado*, and hence the title to the land—at the time owned by friends in San Miguel—would be his.

Brother Xavier Making a Quilt.

At Aelred's death, Christ in the Desert gained possession of La Soledad. Prior Philip had assured Aelred that La Soledad would remain as a monastery in the Benedictine tradition, but the community at Christ in the Desert was too small to establish a formal foundation.

Under Mexican law, religious communities were unable to own property. When Father Aelred died, the problem was solved for the new owners by forming a nonprofit corporation for the purpose of manufacturing and selling art and handmade furniture from the surrounding villages. The property was transferred to the corporation.

At first, the brothers tried to give the property to other monasteries, but there were no takers. Since they couldn't give it away, they realized they had to keep it and continue the work that Father Aelred had started for the local villagers. Brother Christopher and Brother Francisco went to live at La Soledad and work on remodeling the existing buildings with the hope that in time Mexican brothers would come, and a formal foundation could be established. Father Aelred had raised funds to build a school in the neighboring village—most improbably named, "Los Rico"—and in July of 1985 the school was completed. Prior Philip and Abbot Gilbert Jones from the Subiaco Congregation went to Mexico to participate in the blessing of the new building. Thirty children were admitted to the first and second grades, and the school offered literacy classes for teenagers and adults. Brother Francisco became the priest for the Los Rico villagers, and in time he left monastic life to continue his work as a diocesan priest in Mexico.

Sister Mary Joaquín Bitler, a nun of the Sisters of Charity and a good friend of the monks of Christ in the Desert, had already gone to help Father Aelred in 1976. A petite, quiet woman, she was a dynamo of energy. She had established the new Saint Vincent's Hospital in Santa Fe, and served as administrator of the hospital for seventeen years. She "retired" to La Soledad to live a life of more intense prayer and solitude. However, there was not much solitude for her at La Soledad. She started a medical clinic for the area's poor and raised funds for medical supplies, instructed the people in health care and sanitation, and started a food program that supplied them with milk, rice, and flour. She had a suspension bridge built over the river that in rainy weather had separated La Soledad and the clinic from the village, and had a well drilled for the villagers, their first source of clean water. Sister Mary Joaquín, called "Madrecita" by her friends in the village, ran the clinic for twelve years, often alone, later with the help of Brother Francisco.

In 1987 two monks from the Abbey of Tepeyac, Father Ezequiel Bas Luna and Brother Fernando Hool Salazar were the first to settle at La Soledad. Slowly, as the Chama monks could raise funds, the construction continued and was finally completed in 1994—although later, in 2004, a church was added. The monastery includes a library and common room, a guesthouse, and quarters for eighteen monks built around a small cloister garden. Father Ezequiel has replaced Brother Fernando as prior, with eight monks now living in the community.

With the completion of La Soledad, two thriving monastic communities, one in New Mexico, one in old Mexico, have now been built in fulfillment of Father Aelred's dreams.

Sister Mary Joaquín with the Villagers and Monks at La Soledad.

13

Ora et Labora

*I*n a letter to the monks, Mike Richardson recalls the work that he and his fellow guests were asked to take on during an average week in the beginning days of the monastery: "A guest's chores included breaking and hauling several tons of concrete, cleaning two feet of manure from the floor of the goat pens, building lambing pens for the expectant ewes, digging two six-foot craters for outhouses, cleaning cells and bathrooms, sweeping the chapel, loading tons of sand and dirt fill for the guesthouse, and fixing the generator." These chores were in addition to preparing meals, cleaning the ranch house, and shopping for groceries.

Fortunately for today's guests, work expectations are not so stringent. The main buildings have now been completed, the sheep and goats are gone, and the brothers do their own shopping. But a primary difference is that there are many more monks to share the workload than the three or four living at the monastery in those early days.

Still, maintenance of the monastery is a never-ending task: firewood must be cut, help is needed cleaning the guesthouse and convento, the church must be swept, the gift shop needs an assistant, the library books need dusting, the flowers beds are thirsty, and on and on. The brothers make it clear they would greatly appreciate any assistance their guests might offer—every day but Sunday, if they should feel so inclined.

After breakfast one morning back in the early 1990s, as the guests gathered outside the refectory to volunteer for work assignments, Brother André suggested that Brother Benedict could use some help with the monastic laundry. Susan, one of the recent arrivals, enthusiastically volunteered. Since the monks don't tend to mix with their guests, there is little chance, outside of work, to talk with them. Helping one of them with the wash seemed to her a great opportunity to ask questions.

Susan followed Brother Benedict back into the sacrosanct "Monks Only" section of the monastery. The laundry was then in a small adobe building at the edge of the river, that once, twenty years earlier, had been the house of Father Aelred's hired man, Andronico. The building contained a huge, ancient Maytag agitator tub. After several attempts to conquer a roaring, snorting dragon of a generator, Brother Benedict finally got the tub to agitate. Mounted on the side of the tub was a wringer made of two cylinders with a handle for turning. "I hadn't seen such a laundry contraption since I was a child," Susan said, recounting the experience later to her fellow guests.

Susan soon found that Brother Benedict, contrary to the dictum of his saintly namesake regarding silence with the guests, was as eager to talk to an "outsider" as she was to talk to him. She learned that Benedict was from Oklahoma. He had been in the monastery only a short time, and had not yet decided if the cenobitic life was really for him. There was a humorous wistfulness about him, she said, and she wondered if he would last in this austere, remote canyon.

As Brother Benedict scooped up the dripping clothes from the tub, Susan cranked them through the archaic wringer. In between trips from the laundry to the monastic clothesline, Brother Benedict regaled her with humorous tales of life in the canyon. One was of the time when a monk stole into the refectory at night and drank up the Communion wine, staggering around the room and breaking a window. "I guess there's one in every monastery," he said, laughing. Another tale was of his own unseemly behavior the week before at Vigils when he discovered in the dim light of the kerosene lamps that a huge tarantula was crawling over his foot. "My screech really disrupted the solemnities," he said, grinning with delight at the recollection. "One of the brothers was dozing in the back row and nearly fell off his bench.

Postulant Luke in the Laundry.

Susan found she was cranking a most interesting assortment of articles through the wringer. In among the socks and sheets and blue denim tunics with their pointed hoods came such items as a pair of apparently filched towels, one bearing the logo of Hyatt, the other of Sheraton, and a sheet embellished with bright blue and yellow daisies. As she pinned these into the sunny November morning, she wondered which monk had swiped the towels, which one liked to sleep among daisies. She said later that the laundry task reminded her of something she had read the night before when studying the *Rule*. In Chapter 55, Saint Benedict sets forth his edicts on "The Clothes and Shoes of the Brethren": "[I]n ordinary places the following dress is sufficient for each monk: a tunic, a cowl (thick and woolly for winter, thin or worn for summer), a scapular for work, stockings, and shoes to cover the feet." Thorough as the *Rule* is concerning all facets of the monk's life, she thought that perhaps there is one aspect of twentieth century monachism that the good saint did not anticipate. "I would suggest an addendum to Chapter 55," she said, laughing to a group gathered in the guests' Common Room. I would title it: "On the Seemliness of the Monastic Clothesline."

On her next visit to the monastery, Susan noted that Brother Benedict was no longer counted among the brethren.

Some time ago, one guest noticed that the flowerbeds around the guest quarters were struggling under the dead, leftover tangle of winter. Monica, a visitor from Los Angeles, suggested she might weed the beds, but was deterred. Brother Christopher would be coming from Santa Fe in a few days, and he was in charge of the gardens.

As soon as Brother Christopher arrived in the canyon, the chapel suddenly sprouted vases of beautiful flowers. Bunches of wildflowers and chamisa stalks were tastefully arranged in front of the stone altar, and poppies and Shasta daisies from the prior's garden were set before the rough-carved votive statues. The side alcove, presided over by Our Lady of Guadalupe, was adorned with an arrangement of yellow and purple wild columbine.

Alas, Brother Christopher has now passed on, and today his ashes lie in the monastery cemetery. In the years before he became a monk, his name in a former life was, most appropriately, Jack Gardner. At the time of this telling, Brother Christopher was the oldest of the brethren. At seventy-eight, he preferred to spend his winters warmed by the central heating of the Immaculate Heart Seminary in Santa Fe. He complained his arthritis couldn't take the long winter months in a monk's cell heated by only a tiny wood stove. In the guise of Jack

Brother Christopher in his Garden.

Gardner, Brother Christopher spent a quarter century as a banker in Philadelphia. For years he had wanted to become a monk, but had had to wait until his Protestant father died before he could quit the bank and withdraw to the cloister.

Christopher was a wonderfully jovial man and he liked to talk. A great source of monastery gossip was reason enough to pull weeds for the work detail. He spent several hours working with the guests in the warm morning sunshine. Once when asked the name of a certain plant, he answered, "Ya got me, honey." His helper was enamored.

Brother Christopher—he was simply called "Bro" by his confreres, and he called everyone else Bro, sometimes even the women—had his serious side, too. Besides spending his winters basking in the seminary's central heating, he was also a seminary formation director for young men seeking to enter the priesthood. His work involved spiritual and psychological counseling, as well as setting up theological study programs. His good humor turned to sadness when he talked about his students. He was disappointed. He saw a decline in the commitment of the young people who came to him. Certainly—he was quick to assure—some were sincere, devoted young men, intent on preparing themselves to be pastors of a public increasingly in search of spiritual values. But more and more he encountered students who were seeking the seminary as a refuge from the harm done them by abusive, neglectful parents. "They are searching for the perfect father," he said, shaking his white-crowned head, "the father they never had. And of course they won't find him in religion or anywhere else."

Until recently, New Mexico was the location of the Servants of the Paraclete, a national rehabilitation center for errant Catholic clergy who were plucked from their parishes for alcoholism, sexual abuse, and other addictions. Brother Christopher recounted how one of the center's psychiatrists came to the seminary to give his students a series of psychological tests. She was attempting to determine the origin of some of the problems recurring in her priestly patients. The psychiatrist discovered that 80 per cent of the young seminarians she tested were victims of child abuse. "I knew that some of them were very disturbed young people," Brother Christopher said, sadly, "but I never thought there were so many."

One summer a few years ago, the guests found that many of the monks were gone. The prior and two brothers were away at an international conference; others were visiting their families or other monasteries. This meant the few remaining monks were especially eager to enlist their guests to help with the chores. Brother Christian suggested the library could use a thorough dusting, and Jake, one of the visitors, volunteered immediately. The monastery library! Jake told us he had fantasies of the famed *scriptoria* of Cluny and Saint Denis, the Gospels of Lindisfarne, Verdun-sur-Meuse, Sankt Gallen, Monte Cassino, Saint Albans. The Illuminated manuscripts by the Venerable Bede, Alcuin of York, Walafrid Strabol, Benedict of Aniane—scholars of the once-splendid monasteries that of political necessity had bequeathed their treasures to the great libraries of modern Europe.

Jake's bibliophagic fantasies were promptly dashed. Alas, there were no illuminated manuscripts, although the collection of art books was extensive. There were books on every religion, on psychology, theology, history—all that one might expect to find in a monastery library and more. As he moved from shelf to shelf, blowing dust from the ridges at the tops of the pages, he discovered a most eclectic mind had been at work in the selection of the monastic reading materials. Saint Thomas Aquinas' *Summa Theologica* shared alphabetical proximity with *Summer Wildflowers of New Mexico*; Saint Augustine's *Confessions* accompanied those of Jean-Jacques Rousseau, Nat Turner, and Felix Krull. Thomas Merton's *Zen and the Birds of Appetite* shared the "Z's" with Bob Pirsig's *Zen and the Art of Motorcycle Repair*; Julian of Norwich and Hildegard von Rupertsburg complemented Alice Walker's Celie and Virginia Woolf's Mrs. Dalloway. James Joyce's Molly sat on a shelf right above the dissertations of Hans Kung; Teilhard and Tillich shared the "T's" with Thurber; Nietsche, Niebuhr, and Nabokoff (he of *Lolita* and he of *Tijerina and the Courthouse Raid*) had fallen behind a shelf on top of each other. Under "Reference," *The Catholic Encyclopedia* shared a shelf with *The Whole Earth Catalog*. No, the spirit was certainly not Cluniac, but Jake did get a better understanding of the intellectual components of twentieth century contemplative life. "One can only imagine what Saint Benedict would make of such a collection," he said, laughing.

Jake also learned something else: that today, "monk" is a profession that in some senses is like any other. Not only do monks attend international conferences, they have a trade literature to match the most pedantic of professions: *The American Benedictine Review, Pax Quarterly, Cuadernos Monasticos, Aide Inter-Monastaires, Saint Vladimir's Theological Quarterly, Monastic Exchange, Australasian Benedictine Review, Cistercian Studies, Journal of Religion in Communist Lands...* only a partial listing of the journals he discovered on the library shelves.

Could this collection be yet another measure of the need for the professional to be "up on the literature"? There were so many journals on the monastery shelves, Jake could only wonder how a monk could even begin to read them and still find time to contemplate the spiritual needs of the world. The monk's decision to remove to the cloister, to profess before his brothers and God the centuries-old vows of stability and obedience, is his decision to devote his life to us, to pray for us, to effectuate our peace. Let's not forget whose interests are at stake here.

During the week Jake spent at the monastery that summer, he got only half the volumes cleaned. "But I take courage in the amount of dust," he said, when telling later of his bibliophilic adventures. "Apparently the quarterlies do not take up too much of a monk's time, at least not here in the Chama Canyon."

Another guest volunteered to help Brother Philip, who was then the prior of the monastery, scrub down the counters and clean out the cupboards of the monastery kitchen. The owner of a small software company, he was delighted at the chance to question the CEO about the practical side of running a monastery.

From the perspective of a guest, the monastery is place of peaceful order, a harmony exemplified by the ancient tones of the antiphons. For the prior, it is indeed that—*and* a scramble for the money to pay the huge, state-required insurance to cover a guesthouse defined as a hazardous hotel, a hotel with no electricity, with glass kerosene lamps that can break on the floor, and open fires in the oil-drum stoves; a scramble for the money to pay health insurance for the resident monks; the money to buy a new pick-up truck. "The lifespan of a pick-up on the rough on- and off-road terrain of the monastery is about three years at best," the prior said. "It's a challenge to keep the brothers and the guests in wood through the winter and food through the year, for money to repair the inadequate water system and the former goat barn that houses seven of our monks. All this must come from donations," he said, "and from the guesthouse and the gift shop, which sells books, religious articles, and paintings, carvings, weavings, cards, and soap that we make here. And clearly this is not enough. The guests may find the primitive conditions 'charming,' the insurance companies do not. Nor do many of our brothers who must live year after year and winter after winter in the charm. Especially Brother Bernard, who broke his leg on the ice at 4 AM one morning on his way to Vigils."

"We need over three million dollars to fix this monastery," Prior Philip continued. "Not only do we need to repair and upgrade what we have, but we need to build new monks' quarters so the monastery can grow, and we need a new kitchen and a bigger gift shop and a place to counsel guests. So many things. We're putting together a big fund-raising project. We're going all over the country looking for funds. We just can't survive much longer like this."

Subsequent guests discovered that the insurance companies have prevailed. The kerosene lamps and wood stoves are gone from the guesthouse, replaced by gas heaters and battery lanterns. And to better see any wayward tarantulas, electric lights illuminate the chapel in the dark early hour of Vigils. Perhaps not nearly so "charming," but decidedly more practical.

⚘ 14

1980s, 1990s and On

*B*y the 1980s, the monks at Christ in the Desert had begun to think about the comfort of their future life at the monastery. The oldest brother, Christopher, was approaching his seventies, and because of arthritis, was spending his winters in the Santa Fe seminary to escape the cold. The active, primitive life in the remote canyon was exhilarating so long as the brothers were young, but as they grew older, the cold, snowy winters, along with months of mud, were beginning to pose problems. The 1964 buildings were in disrepair, and the monks' quarters, as well as the guesthouse, were still heated with wood stoves. The chapel was so cold in the winter that the Offices had to be held in the convento, although for a while in the 1970s, the brothers walled off the side chapel of the Blessed Sacrament with wood and plastic, forming a temporary wall. It wasn't until 1985 that the monks installed the large wood stoves that are still in the chapel, waiting to someday be replaced by radiant heating in the floor.

In 1983, the brothers contracted with John McHugh, the architect of many New Mexican church restorations as well as for the Santa Fe Opera, to prepare a long-range plan for the development of the monastery. McHugh drew up a ten-year construction schedule to be carried out in phases as funds could be made available. The plan proposed that two lower rooms of the guesthouse should become the gift shop, with a new glass door on the east side for a public entrance. Since the gift shop is a major source of income for the monks, it was important to move it from its location in the original ranch house to be more accessible to visitors. The ranch house could then be used for additional monk cells or guest quarters, and later, when new quarters were built, for offices and a classroom for the novitiate. The craft shops and weaving studio would be expanded, and the convento, which was built in 1971 to accommodate only eight monks, would be expanded to include an infirmary. McHugh proposed relocation of the roads, an upgraded water system, and a footbridge across the river. The last phase would be the construction of a number of small passive solar casitas for the monks, four hermitages across the river, and a comprehensive solar energy plan. A major architectural challenge would be to replace the windows in the upper story of Nakashima's chapel with airtight double-paned glass and to install a solar heating system without altering the chapel's appearance. McHugh's plan would cost an estimated $2,000,000.

The monks set about fundraising once again. And once again their friends offered to help by guaranteeing an $80,000 loan from the Capital Bank of Santa Fe, which allowed the brothers to begin construction immediately. A committee, headed by Al Lobato of Santa Fe, took over the fundraising necessary to retire the loan.

The guesthouse was altered to make room for the gift shop, and the ranch house was converted to living quarters. That was the extent of the money, and, as it turned out, that was just as well. The monks realized that McHugh's plan for scattering new monk cells across the landscape would not solve their problems. The existing cells were already scattered, especially since the brothers had converted the old goat barn a quarter mile up the canyon to house seven more. They would still have to walk through the snow and mud to get to the chapel at 4 am, already a challenge for anyone who was elderly or infirm. Furthermore, the disrepair of the original buildings was so great that the adobe wall of one of the cells caved in on its occupant. Fortunately, he escaped without injury.

To add to their problems, the brothers suddenly realized that their sacred space was not so sacrosanct in the minds of miscreants ever in search of money, perhaps to feed a drug habit. The chapel was robbed of Father Aelred's Navajo rugs and the cloth Brother Jeremy had woven for the altar. The Mayan canoa, which held the candle prayers to the Virgin, was perhaps the most valuable item stolen. And then a couple years later, some guests discovered that their possessions had been taken from the guesthouse. The monks decided that the schedule for the Hours must no longer be posted, since it was a giveaway as to when the guests would be gathered in the chapel, and hence the guesthouse most likely empty.

With the exception of people who work for the brothers, not since the families had lived at the monastery did the monks consider allowing people who were not members of a monastic organization to live on the property. However in 1980, the brothers welcomed Ellen Berg, a woman who wished to live there as a hermit. Ellen and her husband and children had been guests at the monastery in the late 1970s. Later, she felt called by God to become a hermit, and she lived for a year in the Bunkers' "Gatehouse." The following year her husband had a small hermitage added on to the Gatehouse for her. She lived a reclusive life in the new hermitage until 1988, when she left to return to her family. Ellen and her husband have now become founding members of a new religious group.

Before the monks could begin to consider a new set of plans for the monastery development, a government action in the canyon caused the brothers great concern. In 1988 Congress had declared the twenty-six and a half miles of the Chama River from El Vado Dam downstream to Abiquiú Dam to be a "Wild and Scenic River." Again, as with the earlier Wilderness Area designation, this would seem a protection for the monastery. However only the upper reach of the river, from the dam at El Vado down to the monastery, was designated "wild"; the stretch from the monastery to the Abiquiú Reservoir was designated "scenic." What "scenic" means to the Forest Service is "recreational use."

For many years the canyon has been a popular summer playground for rafters who float down the river between the two dams. If the river is low, water is released from El Vado Dam on some weekends for their benefit. The trip down takes one or two days, depending on where the rafters start. The Forest Service was concerned that people were causing destruction of the riparian verge by camping anywhere along the shore and shoving their rafts into and out of the river wherever they pleased.

In 1990 the agency prepared a recreation management plan for the scenic stretch of the river. The plan proposed to improve the road into the monastery and would provide a campground, parking areas, an information center, restrooms, and developed "take out" points for the rafters. A public hearing was held on the draft plan, but was poorly attended. There were some objections from people concerned that the improvements might harm the sense of peace and remoteness of the canyon, but most of the public either didn't know about the draft plan, or didn't realize its implications.

Because of the proposed road improvements, the brothers, tired of trying to maintain the road themselves and tired of being called on to rescue people who were stuck in the mud, were initially in favor of the plan. However, when they realized the size of the campground a mile and a half downstream from them and the proposed car and RV parking lot at a raft take-out point opposite the entrance to Chavez Canyon and touching at the monastery boundary, they became alarmed. They feared their peaceful life would be disrupted by "camera-toting tourists in Winnebagos and RV campers," as one newspaper editorial reported. The terrible road conditions did, indeed, keep down the numbers of the curious from wandering into the monastery. The monks considered that perhaps it was preferable to leave the road just as it was. Since few people had shown up to object at the preliminary public hearing, the Forest Service went ahead with the plans, and to any further complaints, the response was "too late."

It wasn't until bulldozers scoured several acres of the landscape for a 100-car parking lot at the Big Eddy—a point where the river makes a wide turn part way up the canyon between Abiquiú Reservoir and the monastery—that both the monks and an alarmed public determined to protest. The Chama is officially defined as a "navigable river," and therefore under the jurisdiction of the Army Corps of Engineers; hence the Forest Service was required to apply to the Corps for a permit to dredge and fill in the river for the ten-foot by sixty-foot concrete boat ramps at the monastery boundary. The Corps permit would require a public hearing.

In the summer of 1992, an anonymous phone call alerted several people of the upcoming public hearing. The Rio Chama Coalition, a group of concerned citizens, was quickly organized: environmental activists and conservation lawyers; ranchers who used the government-owned canyon lands for grazing; rafters who felt the plan would destroy their experience of the river's natural beauty; friends of the monastery who feared the peace and silence of the canyon would be compromised; and the monks themselves. The management plan supposedly would benefit primarily the rafters, but the rafters were some of the most vociferous opponents. Many felt the "Wild and Scenic" designation was a mistake. Jay Sorensen, a professor at the University of New Mexico and an avid rafting enthusiast, said that the designation of Wild and Scenic River was like "putting a big, national neon sign" at the entrance to the canyon.

Many of the local people were already bitter about government actions on the river. When the Abiquiú dam was proposed in 1963, the plan was met with total opposition from the ranchers; their land was condemned regardless. Some people lost not only their land, but their homes as well; even the local cemetery was submerged. Ghost Ranch lost a third of its property. Now that the dam is built, an ongoing problem is the flooding of downriver acequias by the surges of water periodically released from the dam.

The monks made their newsletter mailing list available to the Rio Chama Coalition, which sent out hundreds of notices of what was afoot, and a call to attend the upcoming public hearing. The night of the meeting in Española, over a hundred angry citizens packed the room. Lieutenant Colonel DeBow, who had come to conduct the meeting from the Albuquerque Corps office, was amazed at the turnout. "I've never seen a meeting like this!" he exclaimed to the crowd. As the testimony commenced, one speaker after another blasted the proposed, sixty-foot boat ramps and, although it was not part of the hearing, the Forest Service's management plan as well. The colonel finally asked the audience for a show of hands of those opposed to the project, and finding no one in favor, called a halt to the proceedings. The permit was not granted.

The Forest Service backed off as well. It was too late to do anything about the huge scar of the Big Eddy parking lot, but the proposed campground was reduced by half and developed to a lesser standard, and a proposed information center wasn't built. The parking at the edge of the monastery wasn't put in, and the road, although somewhat improved, was not upgraded to the level the plan had called for.

The government's concessions mitigated much of the impact that would have occurred if the plan had been implemented as proposed. Nevertheless, even with the lesser facilities now in place, the sense of remoteness the canyon once offered its visitors has forever changed.

But the government wasn't finished with the Chama Canyon. The next year a public hearing was called at Ghost Ranch to discuss the environmental impact statement the Corps had just issued for recreational development at Abiquiú Lake. The proposal was to create an aquatic recreation area similar to that in the southern part of the state at Elephant Butte. Many of the same angry ranchers who had lost their land to the construction of the lake in 1963 were at the meeting to protest, as were the members of the recently formed Rio Chama Coalition, the directors of Ghost Ranch, a monk from Christ in the Desert, and this time an aide from the Senator Domenici's office. The arguments against the proposal were the same as the previous year: bringing RV-loads of traffic to developed tourist facilities at the lakeshore would not only burden the entire Abiquiú area, but ultimately would impact the canyon all the way to the monastery. After all the local hullabaloo, the Corps apparently dropped the project, although it was felt by the meeting participants that the plans were likely put on a shelf back in the Albuquerque office to await presentation at a more propitious time.

❦ ❦ ❦

*N*ow that the renovation of the ranch house and the gift shop was finished, the McHugh plan was scrapped, and the monks decided to work out their own development plan. To solve the problem of scattered living quarters, they decided on a traditional cloister, as in the great European monasteries, with monks' cells enclosing a garden replete with a fountain. One of their Mexican brothers sketched out the design. They would also need a new refectory and kitchen, and the old convento could house a meeting room and an expanded library—the books were already bursting their shelves. Covered passageways were needed to allow the brothers to move out of the rain and cold from their cells to the refectory and kitchen and to the church sacristy. A new gift shop and restrooms should be built near the church. The monks needed an adequate electrical system, and the water system for the monastery needed replacement.

Early in 1992, the noted Santa Fe architect, Philippe Register, was hired to draw up the new plans. Register proposed the construction be carried out in three phases: Phase I would consist of twenty-two new monk cells around a cloister garth, as the monks had suggested. The cloister would be connected to the existing convento by an enclosed hallway, and a wide portal would be built in front of the convento entrance. The monastery would be completely converted to solar power. Phase II would include a new computer room, two infirmary rooms, a parlor, the corridor from the cells to the church, and a new sacristy. Phase III would comprise a laundry, shops, garage, kitchen and refectory, a guest reception area with restrooms and the guest master's office, and a new gift shop. The proposal would cost a mere $3,000,000 if not more. The monks were facing a fundraising challenge as never before.

Bill Cody, vice-president of the Southwestern Region of the Episcopal Church and a friend and frequent visitor to Christ in the Desert, agreed to coordinate the fundraising effort at the national level. In honor of their founder, the monks named the fund drive "The Father Aelred Wall Memorial Campaign." An honorary committee of nineteen members was formed that included the names of the rich and famous—Hollywood celebrities, well-known artists, writers, and entertainers, and lights of the Catholic world. Bob Cook, a lawyer in Boulder, Colorado who had been a novice at the monastery during the 1970s, took charge of fundraising in his home state, and Sister Mary Joaquín, assisted by B. J. Weil of Santa Fe, headed the local effort. Sister Joaquín, who had returned from Mexico in 1989 to live as a hermit at Christ in the Desert—a quite mistaken idea on her part, it turned out—was the arch arm-twister for worthy causes. The committee also included Father Aelred's sister, Mary Alice. The campaign would also raise money to complete her brother's dream of a monastery at La Soledad.

The kick-off event was a luncheon in honor of Sister Mary Joaquín at the El Dorado Hotel in Santa Fe. Honorary Chairwoman, Jane Wyatt, who had just finished performing the lead in the play, *Driving Miss Daisy*, was also the guest of honor. Wyatt was a long-time friend of Father Aelred; her children had attended the school at Portsmouth Priory when Aelred was headmaster.

Española friends held fundraising dinners and Santa Fe friends organized a benefit art auction. In 1993, with the assistance of the Thomas Merton Study Center at Bellarmine College in Louisville, gallery owner Linda Durham, Lew Thompson, owner of a public relations firm, Brother Christian, and artist Robert Kelly (whose Aunt Caroline had arranged the sale of the monastery property to Father Aelred in 1964) put together a show and sale of prints of Merton's photographs to commemorate his death twenty-five years earlier. In 1995, fifty artists were invited to the canyon to paint, draw, or sculpt their impressions of the monastery and its landscape, and their creations were sold as a fundraiser at the Zaplin-Lambert gallery on Santa Fe's Canyon Road.

Some of the early money to come in was a $100,000 grant from a Chicago foundation, which the brothers used for their first project, the renovation of the chapel. Tired of trying to chant the Psalms in the freezing cold—one winter the wood stoves managed to bring the temperature in the chapel from minus 17 degrees to zero—they hired contractor Joe Babcock of Santa Fe to help them insulate the roof, fix cracked trusses, and install thermal glass in the central clerestory section of the chapel.

Implementing the phases of Philippe Register's ambitious plans would take many years, but gradually limited amounts of money became available.

Brother Bernard at Work in the Monks' Courtyard, early 1990's.

The monks repaired the water system that had broken down and left them without fresh water for a week. Back in 1964, Shamrock Drilling had put in a well and water system for Father Aelred, but in the ensuing years no one had bothered to keep a record of the location of the pipes. Hence there was always a blind, harried chase through the underground whenever anything went wrong with the system.

Late in 1994, earth moving began for the 22-cell monk's cloister. At the groundbreaking, a time capsule was placed in a hole in the foundation stone of the new cloister, with the names of the participants in the undertaking. Tierra Amarilla resident and surveyor, Gordon Schlegel, volunteered his assistance, and Española building contractor, Richard Cook, contributed the equivalent of $30,000 of earth-moving work. Under the guidance of the general contractor, Burke Denman and Associates, the monks worked with the crew, and they, with the help of volunteers, did much of the work themselves.

Until this time, the monastery was depending for electricity on a few solar panels—a gift from Ghost Ranch Conference Center—and small generators. These provided enough power for some kitchen appliances, a couple of computers and power tools, and low-voltage lamps in the chapel and in some of the monks' cells. The guesthouse was still lit with kerosene lamps and heated with wood stoves, making it continually difficult to get fire insurance. The nearest electric line was thirteen miles out on the highway, and to run a cable from there would be exorbitantly expensive—estimated at $1.2 million. Even if the line were underground, the installation itself would disrupt the beauty of the canyon environment.

The need for energy to run the construction equipment and for more efficient energy to run the new computers rendered a larger solar field that would power the entire monastery an immediate priority. Over the next two years, the monastery installed a state of the art photovoltaic system capable of 80-kilowatt hours. The system is the largest private solar installation in the state. It consists of twelve tracking collectors with twelve 75-watt modules on each collector that feed 200-pound long-life batteries and inverters. Trackers continually point the modules toward the sun, but at night or under cloudy skies, the batteries store enough energy to last the monastery for three days.

In 1995, the monks were devastated by news of the sudden death of their friend and chief fundraiser, Bill Cody. Who could possibly replace a man capable of talking a stranger on the Albuquerque Shuttlejack into pledging

$30,000 to help build a monastery in a remote canyon of New Mexico? Even without him, however, the work Bill had put into the fundraising effort continued to pay off, and the money kept coming in.

Also in 1995, Philippe Register retired, and another architect, Janice Vascott, was hired to see the project through to completion. Janice was dedicated, as was the contractor, Burke Denman, and the renewable energy consultant, Mark Sardella, to completing the project in the most innovative and environmentally friendly way possible. The monks' cells are wired for computers, and the walls are constructed with straw bales, plastered on the outside with stucco and on the inside with adobe. Water heated by solar collectors on the roofs is stored in a large tank. Domestic water is heated indirectly by the hot water in the tank; hot water for the radiant heating system is pumped directly from the tank to tubes in the flooring of the cells. The cost recovery period for this water system is only eight years; thereafter the system is essentially free.

Friends from the outside were invited to help with the straw-bale construction, and the contractor held three weekend bale-raising workshops. The workshop participants built a lot of walls and had a lot of fun, especially when folks arrived from Española bearing trays of homemade enchiladas.

The environmentally sensitive construction team not only used both passive and active solar energy to light and heat the buildings, and 36,000 square feet of straw bales as the primary building material, but the lumber used throughout the monastery construction came only from sustainable forests. A man-made field of cattails, reeds and other plants that break down solid waste and chemicals—a constructed wetlands—processes the monastery's wastewater. When fully operational, the treated effluent will irrigate a planned fruit orchard.

In 1998 the contractor, Burke Denman, received the Renew America Green Building and Real Estate Development Award for the innovative and environmentally sensitive work at the monastery, as well as for other of the company's projects. Shortly after the award, Denman bowed out and a new contractor, Tom Connor, took over. Yet in a few short years Tom died, and in 2004 the monastery hired another company to finish Phase III—the new refectory and gift shop. The construction effort at Christ in the Desert has become a world model for the use of sustainable resources.

Volunteers Plastering a Straw Bale Wall.

☙ 15

Blessing of the Abbot

This monastery seeks only to keep alive the simplicity of Benedictine monasticism: a communal life of prayer, study, work, and praise in the silence of the desert, where the word of God has always been best heard and most faithfully understood.

—Thomas Merton

We can only wonder what visions Father Aelred may have had for the future of his monastery when he and his friend drove the barely passable road into the Chama Canyon for the first time. Would the changes in the canyon on a September day in 1996 be an answer to his prayers of so long ago? Perhaps he would be amazed to see two hundred or more visitors standing in the unfinished courtyard of the spanking new monks' cloister, waiting in the warm sunshine for the Most Reverend Michael J. Sheehan, Archbishop of Santa Fe, to arrive. The archbishop was coming to bless the new quarters, but more important, he was coming to bestow the abbot's miter on the pate of Dom Philip Lawrence, the newly elected abbot of Christ in the Desert.

Some years ago, Prior Philip explained to his guests the difference between an abbot and a prior. "The abbot needs at least twelve monks who have professed their final, solemn vows," he said. "I have only six. The others are still considering if they are really cut out for monastic life."

With the professions of four brothers at Thanksgiving, 1995, the monastery gained fifteen solemnly professed monks, more than the requisite number needed to request permission from Abbot Gilbert Jones, the abbot president of the Subiaco Congregation, to become an abbey. The request was approved, and on the Feast of Saint John the Baptist the following June—exactly thirty-two years since the monastery was founded—the brothers of Christ in the Desert elected Prior Philip to be their abbot. The Right Reverend Aldhelm Cameron-Brown, the Abbot Visitor from the English Province of the Subiaco Congregation, installed the abbot-elect in the monastery chapel.

It is customary for the archbishop to bless the new abbot, and on that warm September day it was the public ceremony of blessing, the final act of Philip's installation, that had brought the monastery's friends to the canyon.

Archbishop Sheehan's car finally arrived in a cloud of dust, late because of last minute demands in Albuquerque. Wearing a flowing white chasuble, he hurried through the grama grass and chamisa to the courtyard entry, crosier and miter in hand. Inside the new cloister, the friends of the monastery lined the portal walkways eagerly awaiting the start of the ceremony. In a moment, the sound of voices chanting the lines from Psalm 118 swelled through the gates:

Lord, you are just, and the judgments you make are right.
Show mercy when you judge me, your servant.

The archbishop, the abbot-elect, and the brothers in their long white robes solemnly advanced into the dusty garth and took their places: the archbishop at the temporary altar in the center, the monks at the sides of the unfinished yard.

It was a day of great celebration for the brothers of Christ in the Desert. In addition to the archbishop, the Rev. Justin Dzikowicz, Abbot of Saint Paul's Abbey of Newton, New Jersey, was present, as well as Abbot Andrew Miles of New Mexico's Pecos monastery, many religious from other monasteries, and priests from the Santa Fe archdiocese. Philip's parents and his sister and her husband were among the guests, as were Brother Gabriel Duffee and Prior Martin Boler, who had come from Mount Saviour. It was a day for Mount Saviour to celebrate as well, for there had been many years when the New York monks doubted their fledgling foundation would survive.

The long blessing Mass began. Brothers Christian and André presented the abbot-elect to the archbishop, and Brother André, who was the new prior, verified to him that Philip had been duly elected abbot in accordance with Saint Benedict's *Rule*. Then the archbishop examined the intentions of the new abbot: "Will you persevere in your determination to observe the *Rule* of Saint Benedict and will you be diligent in your teaching the brothers to do the same, and so

Abbot's Blessing. From Left: Abbot Andrew Miles, Abbot Philip, Archbishop Michael Sheehan, Abbot Justin Dzikowicz.

encourage them in the love of God, in the life of the Gospel, and in fraternal charity?" To this and to other questions as to the abbot-elect's intentions, Philip responded, "I will." After asking a litany of fifty-six saints, one by one, to pray for the abbot and the assembly, the archbishop presented Philip with a copy of the *Rule,* admonishing him to use it to guide and sustain his brothers "as God gives you strength and human frailty allows." Then he touched Philip's ring, asking him to wear it as the seal of fidelity, placed the miter on the new abbot's head, and handed him the tall, crook-necked pastoral staff. The Mass continued to its conclusion, and with a final *Te Deum* and a sprinkle of holy water to bless the new monks' quarters, the celebration was over. The new abbot, the archbishop, and the concelebrants retreated from the courtyard as the monks sang the *Salve Regina*.

The formalities at an end, everyone was invited to share in a traditional New Mexican feast: tamales, posole, enchiladas, tortillas, beans, and chile—on into the late afternoon.

The monks of Christ in the Desert welcome visitors from all over the world—those of any faith and those of no faith—to seek quiet and peace in the simplicity of their singing, in the beauty of their canyon. For the people of northern New Mexico who came that day to witness the prior become the abbot of the monastery, there was a special sense of ownership. The Monastery of Christ in the Desert is not just for the brothers who live there; it is the people's monastery too, it is in this canyon for them. Many had helped support it, as had the women who prepared the celebration feast that day and for many other celebrations as well, and the many who had responded to the need for funds. Some of the people standing in the cloister garth that afternoon had even helped Father Aelred mix the adobe mud to build the chapel walls; more recently, some had helped to plaster the straw bale walls of the new cloister. And the brothers acknowledge these gifts as they acknowledge their guests' needs and concerns in their daily prayers. This sense of ownership was apparent in the events that September afternoon: the people had come to the canyon to celebrate the coming-of-age of their monastery.

That day marked perhaps the greatest change in the monastery since Father Aelred first envisioned the simple structures he would build in the orange-walled canyon. In the early years of the monastery, Aelred had anticipated that no more than eight to twelve monks would live there. Now the brothers are counted at twenty-five. As with all change, they must guard against loss as they celebrate gain. All social institutions, even monasteries, need to grow or they will wither once the fire of the initial vision dies back. Let us hope that the monastery's new level of importance as an abbey in the Benedictine Order will not diminish that early vision. It is a vision of the simple life so well expressed by Thomas Merton, who stayed at Christ in the Desert in 1968: "This monastery seeks only to keep alive the simplicity of Benedictine monasticism: a communal life of prayer, study, work, and praise in the silence of the desert, where the word of God has always been best heard and most faithfully understood."

16
The Monastery Goes "Online"

Go into the whole
world and proclaim
the Gospel to every
creature.
—Mark 16:15

While the fundraising and construction work continued through the 1990s, the Chama monks were busy on other fronts as well. Always seeking new ways to earn income, in 1993 they established a thrift shop on Saint Michael's Drive in Santa Fe, helping Santa Fe's Rape Crisis Center and subsequently other nonprofits with some of the proceeds. Later, in 2002, they opened the small "Monks' Corner," a shop near the Santa Fe Plaza where they sell crafts, books, and religious articles from Christ in the Desert as well as from other monasteries. In 1996, the brothers bought 40,000 Buckfast bees to start a honey business. Brother Francisco had raised bees ten years earlier, but no one took them over when Francisco left to stay at La Soledad. The new bees lived in two beautiful hives that Brother Marcelo designed and decorated for them, and for a while the monks had delicious wild-flower honey on their breakfast toast. As a business, however, the project never got off the ground and came to a sorry end some years later when a bear tore apart the entire operation.

In 1995, Christ in the Desert decided to go "online." It seemed an excellent means to sell items from the gift shop, to book reservations for the guesthouse, and provide essays on monastic life and spirituality. The previous year had brought twelve new vocations to the monastery, doubling the total to twenty-four, and the brothers had to find a significant new source of income to cover the added expense. Brother Mary Aquinas, formerly a systems analyst in Denver, conceived the idea that the monks could make a good living as Web site designers. After all, media design in some form had been the province of monasteries for hundreds of years, and the activity promised to be one that would allow the monks to work without leaving the confines of the cloister. Brother Marcelo, an accomplished artist, designed the monastery's Web site with colorful drawings reminiscent of medieval illuminated manuscripts, and advertised the availability of such Web site designs as a business of the monastery. The site also showed pictures of the monks at work and prayer, sound clips of Gregorian chant, notes on Benedictine history, and "Brother URL" who took the viewer on a tour through the monastery. There was also a contact link for prayer requests.

Before long, the brothers found themselves the object of a nation-wide media blitz. Articles about the new "scriptorium" in the New Mexico desert were noted on ABCNews, MSNBC, the Sunday *New York Times, USA Today, Life Magazine,* and *The New York Times Book Review. Time Magazine* made the scriptorium its cover story. Microsoft donated fifteen new computers and thousands of dollars in software, and Yahoo decreed www.scriptoria.org a "cool site."

The brothers were amazed at how many "hits" their site received—at its peak, 10,000 an hour. Prayer requests poured in, although one disgruntled woman emailed: "I don't want to know anything about your shady religious dealings." The server couldn't handle the volume. At the time, one service provider connected all of New Mexico to the Internet, and at one point the intense demand on the monastery site crashed the whole state. Brother Aquinas had great hopes that the monastery would land a contract to develop a site for the Vatican. Although the brothers did do some work for Rome, they did not get the major contract they had hoped for.

Until 1996, when the monastery installed the new solar field, this entire computer operation was running off a few solar panels, a generator and a single, temperamental cell phone—at exorbitant cost in phone bills. With the installation of the new solar array, however, solar electricity was running all the computers, satellite phones and kitchen appliances, the pumps for the water system, and all the construction equipment for building the monastery.

There were so many orders for design services that what at first seemed the perfect answer for work that would not interfere with the contemplative

The Computer Room.

life, soon began to take over that life. In the days when monks were hand-copying and illustrating ancient texts in their medieval *scriptoria,* time was not an issue; they had the market cornered. In today's world, the market is competitive, and time is measured in deadlines. Designing Web sites may be appropriate to monastic seclusion, it is not appropriate to the monastic sense of time. Although the Web site orders were bringing in good money, before long the abbot called a halt. Today, the monastery's Web site, which has changed its address to www.christdesert.org, takes registrations for the guesthouse, sells books and craft items from the gift shop, presents the abbot's homilies and note book for past weeks, and provides information about Benedictine history and monastery activities. There is still a link for prayer requests. Brother Marcelo, the master "illuminator" of the Web site, has left monastic life, as has Brother Mary Aquinas.

But Aquinas has not left the Web. Impressed by the number of people seeking spiritual help on the monastery's site, he has developed his own online service called nextSCRIBE. Aquinas believes the Catholic Church must take advantage of the digital medium to reach out, not only to Catholics, but to everyone who is hungry for spiritual help. He reminds us that in the 1500s, when Rome wanted to suppress Protestant ideas, the printing press continuously produced copies of Martin Luther's ninety-five theses, far outpacing the pope's agents' ability to destroy them. Not that Brother Aquinas wants to use the internet as an ideological weapon; rather, he stresses that just as Luther once used the new medium of the printing press to spread his ideas, the Church must recognize the importance of the new medium of the World Wide Web as a powerful tool for helping individuals who seek a spiritual cognizance that they cannot find in more traditional venues. As Aquinas describes his site: "The focus is not just on the technical religious terminology, it's on beauty and truth and the goodness …on leading a life dedicated to love."

🦢   🦢   🦢

*J*ust as Father Aelred many years earlier had been eager to establish a monastery in the Chama Canyon that would celebrate a "return to the sources," in 1994, a monk in vows to the Oregon monastery of Mount Angel, wanted to establish a monastery in Mexico that would also strictly follow the tenets of the *Rule.* Father Thomas Mitchell approached Christ in the Desert to sponsor a second Mexican foundation. La Soledad was not yet completed, and the monks agreed to the request on condition they would not be financially responsible for the new effort. Mount Angel allowed Father Thomas to transfer his vows to the Chama monastery, and in 1997, Archbishop Obeso-Rivera of Vera Cruz blessed the cornerstone of Christ in the Desert's new foundation of Santa Maria y Todos los Santos near Xalapa in the state of Vera Cruz. Although the brothers do provide some limited financial help, the twelve monks at Todos los Santos earn their living primarily from their gift shop and guesthouse, along with fundraising and various agricultural activities.

Soon there was another foundation request, this time from Chicago. In the past few years, Chicago's parishes had begun losing membership, and the number of priests as well as the parochial finances were becoming increasingly limited. The diocese determined that several of the parishes should be combined, and this left a number of empty churches. Many of these properties were sold, but in 1991 Cardinal Joseph Bernardin, the archbishop of the Chicago diocese, offered one of these churches, along with an adjacent convent and parking lot, to a small group of men in Minnesota who wished to form a monastic community. The monks moved to Chicago and—after spending several days clearing out a churchful of stored gym equipment and library books—set up their monastery in what had previously been the Immaculate Conception Parish Church on Chicago's Near South Side. The monks approached Christ in the Desert to sponsor them as a foundation. Again, as with Todos los Santos, the Chama brothers were willing so long as they would have no financial responsibility for the community.

As a foundation of Christ in the Desert, the monks of the Monastery of the Holy Cross of Jerusalem, as do the monks of La Soledad and Todos Santos, make their professions of vows to the Chama monastery. The Holy Cross brothers support themselves selling burial urns and caskets, as well as managing a successful bed and breakfast and a retreat/guesthouse. In 2005, the community had six brothers in final vows, and a novice planning to make his temporary vows.

The deserts of Mexico and the Southwest of the United States are closely related historically, geographically, spiritually, and in many ways, culturally; on the other hand the city of Chicago seems far from a New Mexican's idea of a desert. But for Christians, the desert has always been a place of both satanic seduction and spiritual redemption. The Chicago brothers call their city an "urban desert," a place where the satanic forces are crime, homelessness, poverty, and alienation. The Monastery of the Holy Cross of Jerusalem, located in the Bridgeport neighborhood, just south of Chicago's downtown Loop, is a place of quiet and prayer and hospitality in this urban desert, a place of "silence in the city," as the monks describe their monastery.

Monastery of the Holy Cross of Jerusalem, Chicago.

Monastery of Santa Maria y Todos los Santos.

☙ 17

Our Lady of the Desert

*A*side from the ongoing construction in the 1990s at Christ in the Desert, which, when completed, will transform the monastery grounds, a most significant change for the brothers of the Chama is the sponsorship of a women's community. In 1989, two oblates of the monastery, Jacqueline Nelson and Susan McClaine, petitioned the Archdiocese of Santa Fe for permission to form a women's community and live according to the *Rule,* as at Christ in the Desert. Archbishop Sánchez agreed to the women's request on condition that Prior Philip oversee them. The next year, on February 2, 1990, the Monastery of Our Lady of the Desert was formally established, and Prior Philip blessed the two oblate women in the Chama chapel. Jacqueline became Sister Elizabeth and Susan, Sister Anne.

Soon a nurse from Albuquerque, Theresa Serna, joined the two, and became Sister Mary Benedicta. The women lived for a while in a rented house near the village of Abiquiú and then moved to a house in Santa Cruz on two acres with space for two guest rooms and a chapel. Although the brothers supported them financially, the sisters took in guests and, as their brothers had earlier, learned to weave. Sister Elizabeth, a gifted artist, painted retablos and icons.

Once again, Prior Philip called on the monks' friend, Sister Julianne, for help. Concerned that the three women didn't fully understand what they were getting into and that they needed an experienced teacher, he asked Julianne to take over the women's instruction and to be their superior. Julianne, busy with her work in Fort Worth as the financial manager for her community, the Western Province of the Sisters of Saint Mary of Namur, told him she couldn't leave her job. The two finally compromised, however, and agreed that Sister Julianne would be the prioress of Our Lady of the Desert, but would come from Fort Worth to teach the oblates for only a week each month. Apparently her instruction as to the rigors of a life-long commitment to the Benedictine way was so forceful that both Sisters Elizabeth and Anne departed. Over the next two years several women came and left, until finally the last aspirant pulled out of the driveway to seek a different life, and Sister Benedicta was left alone.

Sister Benedicta, who tells us she had never lived alone before, was overwhelmed suddenly to be left to try to keep the little monastery alive on her own. But she held out for a year, occasionally having guests spend the night, and now and then entertaining brothers who would stop in to visit while in town for a shopping trip or a medical appointment. She continued weaving placemats and runners to sell in the monastery gift shop, and every day faithfully celebrated the Divine Office all by herself in the little Santa Cruz house. Benedicta relates that her neighbors were grateful to hear the bell ringing, especially during Desert Storm, because they knew she was offering prayers for them and for all the world.

Finally a year later, in 1993, Sister Placida Fisher (she later changed her name to Sister Mary) joined her. Placida had spent eight years as a nun in Arizona, but felt drawn to the contemplative life at the little monastery. For the next few years, except for Julianne's monthly visits, no one else joined them. Weekdays, the two women attended Mass at Santa Cruz, and on Fridays, drove to Christ in the Desert to take part in formation classes with the brothers; on Sundays they drove again to the canyon to attend Mass. Eventually two women from the Philippines joined them, Sister Scholastica Floro and Sister Amelita Salvador.

In 1997 the Santa Cruz house was sold, and the women moved to the ranch house on the Chama property. Sister Julianne completed her work in Fort Worth, and ultimately she, too, came to live in the ranch house. Before moving from Santa Cruz, the sisters had decided that their two cats, Moses and Jerry, should be given away to friends; they worried the cats wouldn't be safe from wild animals in the canyon. Immediately after delivering them to their friends, the sisters received a phone call that the cats had disappeared. A bedraggled Moses took only four days to make the five miles back to the Santa Cruz house, and three days after that, Jerry arrived. Alas, Jerry didn't survive two weeks in the canyon, but eight years later Moses is still roaming the wilds, stopping in to the women's little monastery now and then for dinner.

By now, in addition to the prioress, there were three sisters in the group: Amelita, Benedicta, and Mary. Sister Scholastica had decided the canyon was too cold for her, and left to pursue her vocation in sunnier climes. Three of the women lived in the ranch house, and Sister Mary was in a tent—until it blew away. The goat barn, which had first housed Father Aelred's misbegotten goats, then the sheep and four cows, then a pottery, eventually a laundry and

Monastery of Our Lady of the Desert.

carpentry shop, then ten brothers, was once again renovated——this time into room for seven sisters, a chapel, a kitchen/refectory, and a small visitors' parlor. In December, 1997, the women moved in.

An early guest at Our Lady of the Desert was Mira Nakashima, the daughter of George Nakashima, the architect of Christ in the Desert's chapel. Like her father, Mira is also a woodworker; as a gift for the women's new chapel, she designed and built an altar.

Sister Julianne remarked once to a reporter that the hardest thing she could imagine is living in community. "Often the people you encounter are not those you would choose as friends in the outside world. The only way to deal with this is to focus on God, and on why it is you are here." The sisters of Our Lady of the Desert have the added challenge of isolation in the remote canyon wilderness. Julianne commented that sometimes a guest would feel so anxious that the canyon was closing in, that he or she would have to be driven out.

Certainly living together in a community of members from diverse nations is a challenge. Not only do the nuns have to understand the cultural differences of their sisters, those who wish to join the community must sometimes wait for years to obtain a visa to immigrate to the United States. Sister Guadalupe Poonoose's visa came through by divine intervention. A nurse from Kerala, Guadalupe knew it was next to impossible to get a visa to allow her to emigrate from India. Nevertheless, at each quirk of the bureaucratic process she prayed to the Virgin of Guadalupe, and in record time the Virgin came through for her. Sister Hilda Tuyuc's visa to permit her to leave Guatemala had been held up for three years. Together with Brother Christian, Sister Julianne went to the American consulate in Guatemala City. Wearing her sternest high-school-principal face, she informed the consul that Sister Hilda's presence in the United States was solely in the interest of serving God. The face must have sufficiently impressed the consul, for abruptly everything was straightened out.

By 1999, Sister Julianne and Abbot Philip felt that it was time for the sisters to find an existing monastery that would take them on as a foundation and provide them with canonical status. By this time Sisters Hilda from Guatemala, Guadalupe from India, Maria Teresa from Vietnam and Kateri from Albuquerque had joined the group, and the sisters built a separate structure of eight new cells adjacent to the renovated goat barn.

Sisters of Our Lady of the Desert, 2005.

Sister Julianne contacted her home house in Belgium, the Sisters of Saint Mary of Namur, to see if the Belgian nuns would be willing to sponsor the new monastery. The Belgian superior felt it would be more appropriate for the Chama sisters to look for a specifically Benedictine contemplative order. Through the Subiaco Congregation, the women found the Monastery of the Presentation of Our Lord in the Temple, located at Jamberoo, Australia. The monastery—called simply "Jamberoo"—sent two nuns to visit the sisters at Our Lady of the Desert to determine if the Australian monastery should accept them as a foundation.

Despite the thousands of miles that separate the Chama Canyon from Australia, the Jamberoo sisters voted unanimously to sponsor the women. The Chama nuns started a canonical novitiate under two visiting sisters, Antonia Curtis and Maureen Therese Woodhouse, from Jamberoo. The next year four of the sisters made their temporary vows to the distant abbey. On February 2,

2005—the Feast of the Presentation in the Temple and the founding date of Our Lady of the Desert fifteen years earlier—Sisters Mary Benedicta, Hilda, and Mary made their final, solemn vows of obedience, stability, and conversion of life in front of their families and friends in the chapel at Christ in the Desert. Sister Antonia, the delegate of Mother Abbess Benedicta of Jamberoo, accompanied by Sister Maureen Therese accepted the vows of the three, and also accepted Sister Julianne's vows that she was now making as a Benedictine, completing the transfer of her perpetual vows from the Sisters of Saint Mary of Namur to the Australian abbey.

After the acceptance of the vows, the four women sang the *Suscipe* three times, asking the Lord to receive them. Then they lay on the floor and were covered with a funeral pall to symbolize the death of their previous lives. After a long invocation, or "litany of saints," Sister Antonia called the women to their rebirth.

Sister Julianne has retired as prioress of Our Lady of the Desert; Sister Benedicta has been appointed to replace her. As Mother Mary Benedicta, she is now the superior of ten nuns. She has come far in her vocation from the year she spent frightened and alone in the oblate house in Santa Cruz.

Our Lady of the Desert has its own Constitutions that follow those of Jamberoo. The sisters are working toward economic self-sufficiency, although for now their main support must come from Christ in the Desert. Sister Hilda is a weaver, and sells her work at the Ortega's weaving shop in Chimayó. Sisters Teresa and Elizabeth sew habits, and the American sisters make readings on tapes for shut-ins and teach English as a Second Language to the foreign nuns. With the recent addition of the eight new cells, the nuns are able to accommodate some guests.

According to Abbot Philip, the long-range plan for Our Lady of the Desert provides for a completely new monastery with a guesthouse and gift shop to be built on the property acquired from the Brosseaus across the river. The proposed guesthouse and shop, along with the sisters' other activities, should provide sufficient income for them to become financially independent. But this will have to wait until the work is completed at Christ in the Desert, and a bridge across the Chama can be built. In time, the Sisters of Our Lady of the Desert hope to become an autonomous monastery—one day to become an abbey.

Mother Mary Benedicta, Prioress of Our Lady of the Desert.

❦ 18

A New Kind of Monastery

If you don't find God in the next person you meet, it's a waste of time looking for him further.

—Mohandas Gandhi

By the turn of the millennium, the construction at Christ in the Desert still wasn't completed, although the new monks' quarters were occupied and the corridors to the old refectory and the church sacristy were in place. Brother Xavier's tiny hermitage upriver had been wired for electricity and plumbed for hot and cold running water. (Brother Denis, the Trappist monk who built the primitive stone tower back in the 1960s, would be amazed to see how "modernized" it has become.) Also a hermitage near where Sister Mary Joaquín had lived was constructed at the southern end of the monastery near the river. The original guesthouse was converted from kerosene lamps to battery-charged flourescent lanterns, the woodstoves replaced by gas heaters, and a new bathroom for women added. Juan Gallegos's old ranch house was renovated to accommodate additional guests.

By 2004, the new refectory and the new gift shop were finally finished, but the powerhouse for electricity was still not ready, hence the County would not grant the monks a certificate of occupancy. Lack of electricity, however, was never a problem for the Chama brothers who had lived for years without such conveniences. They moved into their new refectory for daylight celebrations—Brother

Original Guesthouse, designed by George Nakashima.

Dominic's ordination and the professions of the sisters of Our Lady of the Desert—bringing the celebration feast in from the old kitchen.

The new refectory, gift shop, and reception area reflect the concern for aesthetics that has characterized Christ in the Desert since Father Aelred hired George Nakashima to design the striking chapel and commissioned the artists who created the paintings, sculptures, and handmade rugs with which he furnished the monastery buildings. Over the years the monks have been recipients of several works of art: the large paintings of St John the Baptist and Saint Benedict by Bob Lenz in the old refectory along with the *Cristo* by Gerald Bonnette, and several pieces by *santero* Ben Ortega, including the tall wooden Saint Francis in the guesthouse garden. The twin brothers from Argentina, Claudio, as carver, and Marcelo, as painter, produced the statue of Saint John the Baptist in the chapel while staying at the monastery in the 1990s. The large *Cristo* that hangs on the wall of the chapel was carved by the Taos *santero,* Victor Goler, and the scenes depicted on the doors of the Blessed Sacrament were truly a community effort by many of the artist brothers of the monastery. In the new guest reception area, a large fresco of the head and shoulders of Christ by artist Joe Ramirez of Chicago evokes the Byzantine style of iconic mosaics. To visitors who enter the reception area, Christ appears to bless them from the wall. There is a subtle background of Italian landscape behind the Christ figure, as in paintings by Renaissance artists.

On the back wall of the refectory, a huge mural painted by Father Damian Higgins from Georgia—who also painted the image of the Virgin in the chapel—depicts the "Hospitality of Abraham and Sarah," based on Genesis 18. There are three angels visiting the couple, interpreted as an Old Testament prefiguration of the Holy Trinity. On either side is a line of figures representing saints who have played significant roles in the history of monasticism: Saints Benedict and his sister Scholastica, Saints Francis and Clare who are patrons of the Santa Fe archdiocese, Saint Mary and Saint John the Baptist, Kateri Tekawitha, the blessed of the Native Americans, and Blessed Juan Diego of Mexico.

Most spectacular is the large expanse of stained glass that covers the entire gable of the new refectory in a wide-based triangle from the top of the wall to the peak of the roof, a gift from a friend of the monks, and designed by Santa Fe glass artist Margaret Nelson. During the day, the strident forms of brilliant color play upon the walls and floor of the refectory, much as do the stained glass windows of Henri Matisse's Chapelle du Rosaire in the French town of Vence, the inspiration for the Chama window.

Work on the monastery's two Mexican foundations progressed as well in 2004. Abbot Philip and the Bishop of Celaya presided over the blessing of the new church at La Soledad, and at Santa Maria y Todos los Santos, the new monks' quarters were completed.

Up until the time that the brothers embarked on the major Father Aelred Wall Campaign to fund the new buildings, Christ in the Desert had managed to pay off all its debts. Of course, what was initially proposed as a $3 million project in 1992 by 2005 had become an $8 million-plus project, and the brothers were in debt for a million dollars. Part of this amount could be met with pledges from their friends. The conversion of the old refectory and kitchen, which was anticipated for the expansion of the library and for a community meeting room, would have to wait a while. Now would be a time for fundraising to deal with the debt.

Cloister at Nuestra Señora de la Soledad.

Once the construction debt is finally paid, the monks still must find economic projects that will allow them to become self-sufficient for their daily operational needs. The guesthouse and gift shop have provided much of their income in the past, but with a current population of twenty-five monks (on occasion there have been as many as thirty), plus lay members and visitors, the brothers are searching for new sources of income. Whatever those sources will be, they still must allow the monks to maintain their contemplative life within the confines of the monastery. Currently they are looking into several possibilities: part ownership of a brewery to be developed near the Pecos Monastery; marketing fruit preserves under the Christ in the Desert name; a guesthouse for the sisters to provide them with a steady income. No matter what the future brings in relation to these specific ideas, new projects must continue to be developed: the monastery has grown beyond the point that it can survive on the largess of its friends and the donations of its visitors.

The year 2002 brought great sadness to the brothers: for the first time they lost one of their own to death. Brother Christopher had come from Mount

Saviour in the early years of the foundation. He had watched the floundering new monastery, struggling at times with as few as two or three monks, grow to the status of an abbey, with twenty-five members and a spanking new set of monastic buildings. Christopher was the monk with the green thumb, who cultivated the flowers that graced the chapel altar and the refectory in the summertime. Brother Edward, reminiscing about the two years he spent at Christ in the Desert in the 1970s, remembers Brother Christopher's flowers next to the black bowl made by the famous San Ildefonso potter, Maria, set at the base of the stone altar. For Edward, the arrangements remain as a vivid impression. Christopher was always a grateful friend to the guests, many of whom volunteered to help him in his gardens.

Christopher's death was followed by another loss for the Chama brothers. Not a monk, but for many years a resident of the monastery and certainly a beloved participant in the community, Sister Mary Joaquín died in 2003 at her motherhouse of the Sisters of Charity in Ohio. After the twelve years she spent at La Soledad helping Father Aelred and the people of Los Rico, she withdrew to a hermitage at Christ in the Desert to live out her years—or so she imagined. She was immediately commandeered to head up the Father Aelred Wall fundraising campaign that would ultimately pay for the new construction at the monastery. She continued to live at Christ in the Desert until shortly before her death.

Sister Mary Joaquín's work in Los Rico was preceded by seventeen years as the administrator of Saint Vincent's Hospital in Santa Fe. An acclaimed citizen of the City of the Holy Faith, she transformed a small Catholic hospital into a modern health care facility. During her tenure, the hospital added a coronary care unit and a nuclear medicine department, and she lobbied for Santa Fe County to establish an indigent fund for patients unable to pay. The old Catholic hospital she inherited on Palace Avenue near the Plaza was a wreck. The equipment was poor, the basement flooded when it rained, and daily the elevator would get stuck. Mary Joaquín was the last nun to head the Santa Fe hospital that her Order had established in 1865. She arranged for the construction of the modern regional facility on Saint Michael's Drive, and under her guidance the hospital was converted from a Catholic institution to a nonprofit community corporation. Firmly opposed to labor unions, Mary Joaquín had a reputation as a tough administrator; yet her employees—if sometimes disagreeing with her stand against unions—respected her, and knew they could count on her to treat them fairly. Twice she was voted "Citizen of the Year" by the Santa Fe Board of Realtors, and Mayor Joseph Valdez proclaimed

October 17, 1976 to be "Sister Mary Joaquín Day." When a reporter for the *Santa Fe New Mexican* asked her to talk about her success as an administrator, she replied, "Always make right turns, never left turns. It will keep you out of trouble."

🖋️   🖋️   🖋️

When the Monastery of Christ in the Desert joined the Subiaco Congregation in 1983, the brothers immediately became part of a greater world of international monasticism. Previously they had had some contact with Mexican monks through their relation with Father Aelred and his work at La Soledad. But the Subiaco Congregation, through its nine National Provinces brought the brothers into contact with Benedictine monasteries around the world. The English Province of the Congregation, of which Christ in the Desert is a member, has both monks and nuns in five countries: England, Ghana, the United States, Scotland, and Mexico. At once the Chama brothers were able to visit other monasteries in the province for extended stays for educational opportunities and to provide assistance as needed. In turn, members of these monasteries were able to visit Christ in the Desert and participate in the brothers' contemplative life. Because of the Subiaco connection, Our Lady of the Desert has attracted nuns from other countries and was able to find their Australian Jamberoo sponsors.

Before long, the brothers of Christ in the Desert found that monks from around the world were interested in permanently joining their monastery. They have welcomed monks from Argentina, South Africa, Mexico, Italy, Taiwan, India, the Philippines, Vietnam, and England. Today, some are still present in the Chama community, some have left to return to their home countries or to other monasteries, some have left to pursue other directions in their lives.

In 1988, the Vietnamese government became somewhat more open to information from the United States, and the monks began sending their newsletter to the Vietnamese monasteries that are members of the Subiaco Congregation. The superiors of Thien Binh and Thien Phuoc monasteries responded. The abbot of Thien Binh asked if the Chama brothers would be willing to take two of his monks. There is tension between the communist government and the Catholic Church, especially those Catholics who seek

Ordination of Brother Dominic, 2004.

monastic life in Vietnam. There can be political troubles for a monk or a nun with a family member who worked for the South Vietnamese government or for the Americans during the war.

Over the last years, five brothers have come from Vietnam to live in the New Mexico community. In 1995, Brothers Mayeul and Andrew made their solemn vows, and in 2004, Brother Dominic was ordained to the priesthood in the monastery chapel by Archbishop Sheehan and Bishop Joseph of Hai Phong. Today, three of the five monks from Vietnam are priests.

The monastery on the Chama has become an international community. At this time, two-thirds of the monks are not native-born Americans. While the brothers' exposure to many different cultures is stimulating, it also brings many questions and challenges. For example, English is the language of the monastery and it is essential that the foreign monks learn English. The question arises: When is it appropriate for a monk to speak his own language with those who understand it, when others do not? For some it is difficult to learn English—

should they be expected to learn Latin as well? The Mass and readings at the monastery are spoken in English, but much of the Gregorian music is now sung in Latin. Many of the monks are far from their families and the cultures of their birth. Some may feel frustrated by an initial inability to communicate. Adjustment to a new language, to unfamiliar foods, to a new landscape and environment can be stressful. As a foreign monk experiences this period of acculturation, much patience and understanding is required of the community as a whole.

🦋 🦋 🦋

*T*here have been so many people who have helped the monks over the years that it is impossible to list them all. If some are not mentioned here, it is hoped they will not take it amiss as neglect or lack of appreciation. One of the most loyal friends has been Jane Serna of Española, along with her sisters Annadelle Sánchez and Betty Norris. These three have organized the many fundraisers that have raised thousands of dollars to help provide income for the brothers. Jane and Brother Jeremy initiated the fundraiser dinners some twenty years ago, selling tickets, and for the first dinner, raffling a donated diamond ring. Soon Aaroney Murphy came to help them, and subsequent fundraisers were held at Florence Jaramillo's Rancho de Chimayó, at the Martinez Hall in Hernandez, at Española Mayor Richard Lucero's home, and as the fundraisers grew in attendance, at Anthony's Restaurant. Jane and her sisters have provided and cooked the food for many of the special occasions at the monastery, such as the profession of vows, the abbot's blessing, and Thanksgiving and Christmas dinners. Every Wednesday Brother Joseph Gabriel stops by Jane's house to pick up food for the monastery that has been collected from various generous donors. Summers, the brothers are welcome to pick fruit and vegetables from their friends' orchards and gardens. Katie Meyers of Albuquerque has helped Jane with the cooking, and she and her late husband, Eddy, were often on call to take the brothers to and from the Albuquerque airport.

Among the earliest friends of Father Aelred and his monks were, and still are, the Discalced Carmelite nuns of Santa Fe. Cloistered, they live a life of prayer and solitude that has been a source of inspiration and support to the Chama brothers. Mother Prioress Rose Teresa and her band of ten or so sisters have enjoyed visits and talks by the monks through the years. Sometimes the brothers celebrate early morning Mass in Santa Fe with the women,

Sogyal and Dugsay, Two Bön Visitors from India.

accompanied by Gregorian chant, which is the heritage of both communities. The nuns of the Carmel of the Sacred Heart of Jesus and Saint Teresa have been a part of the contemplative monastic tradition in the Archdiocese of Santa Fe since 1945.

From the beginning of the foundation, the brothers have maintained a close relationship with their Protestant friends a few miles away at Ghost Ranch Presbyterian Conference Center, exchanging opportunities for teaching and participating in each other's events. They have hosted ecumenical gatherings with Ghost Ranch, and have conducted program exchanges with Dar al Islam, the Muslim community in Abiquiú.

Their most exotic ecumenical exchange was undoubtedly the month-long visit in 2000 by Dugsay Tenzin and Sogyal Thakali, two Tibetan Bön monks from Himachal Pradesh in India. The two young monks speak English, and the Benedictines and the Böns met daily to listen to each other and to discuss such different religious concepts as reincarnation and the Christian transubstantiation. Dugsay and Sogyal quickly became participants in the community life at Christ in the Desert, living with their American brothers in the cloister, daily celebrating the Hours of the Divine Office, taking on a share of the monastery chores, and learning to work on the computer.

Bön is the indigenous religion of Tibet, incorporating many elements of Buddhism, but with a different canon. Bön monks follow a much older founder than the Buddha Shakyamuni. There has been prejudice against the Bön by other Tibetans who wrongly accuse them of shamanism and blood sacrifice. (During the Reformation, Catholics were accused of the same by some of their more fanatical enemies.) The Dalai Lama has done his best to dispel such prejudices among his followers. The Bön monastery in Tibet was destroyed by the Chinese in 1959, and the monk, Menri Trizin Rinpoche—later to become abbot of the re-established monastery of Menri in India—fled to Europe. He spent his early years of exile pursuing Western studies at the University of London and teaching Tibetan culture both in London and at the University of Oslo. He also spent time traveling in Europe, visiting Catholic and Orthodox churches and monasteries, exchanging ideas with the abbots and monks, and meeting with the pope. Because of his experiences in the West, the abbot wanted his monks to learn about Christian monasticism and the manner in which the *Rule* of Saint Benedict is adapted to contemporary monastic life. "We all have a spiritual goal," the Bön abbot said, "we all want to go somewhere, but how do we get there? We have to dialog with each other about the clearest, shortest, simplest way to get there."

Dugsay and Sogyal had spent three weeks at the Abbey of Gethsemani in Kentucky before coming to New Mexico, but they told Abbot Philip that they especially enjoyed their visit at Christ in the Desert because the brothers joked with them. The two monks had never met a Christian before their trip, so it was a new experience for everyone. To keep up this important contact, in 2001 Abbot Philip took Brother Isaac and Brother Dominic to visit the Abbot of Menri in Dolanji, India, and the next year, Brother Joseph Gabriel also visited the abbot.

In early November, 2004, the Bön abbot came to visit Christ in the Desert with three of his young monks. He spoke to the Chama brothers of his religion, and told the story of their exile from Tibet and the re-establishment of the monastery in India. He explained the vows taken by Bön monks and nuns, and told them a little of his own life and monastic journey. These brothers from opposite sides of the world hope to continue their dialog over the years.

❦　❦　❦

*F*rom its beginnings in 1964 as a collection of tents set up along the Chama River by three New York monks with a dream, the tiny monastic settlement of Christ in the Desert has evolved into a substantial abbey with a brotherhood of international monks and with connections to monasteries and other religious groups across the world. This evolution has not been easy. There were times when the effort almost failed: the lack of funds; the conflicts among the brothers and frustrations in attempting to build a community; the lack of perseverance on the part of its earliest members; and at times, the destructive assaults of the New Mexico weather.

Now that the brothers have almost completed their ambitious construction program, some nostalgically lament the loss of a primitive earthiness that characterized life in the early years of the monastery. Nevertheless, they are quick to add that it is indeed a pleasure not to run out of kerosene before they finish reading a chapter, or not to have to trudge through mud and snow to get from their cells to the chapel. Certainly no one complains about the modern bathrooms with hot water and with radiant heat under foot. And they also acknowledge that since the decision to become an international community, the growth of the monastery has permitted opportunities for a deeper, more comprehensive spiritual life than they previously could have imagined.

The new monastic buildings are indeed beautifully designed. They are practical for contemporary monastic life, and yet consciously reflect centuries of Benedictine tradition. Still, no matter how elegant the new buildings or how spectacular the numinous, rock-walled river canyon, it takes more than a beautiful environment to create a monastery. A monastic community takes many years to develop into a cohesive whole, into a communality of outlook that can deal with the inevitability of conflict and at the same time can respect and reflect the individuality of each of its members. As Abbot Philip pointed out in a recent Internet communication, "It is not just the buildings that must be built, it is the total formation of a community so that it becomes the face of Christ for all who visit the monastery."

The challenge that the culturally diverse Chama monks must face in learning not only to accept, but to love their brothers from different cultures with different languages and habits, is merely the monastic version of the challenge

The Monks' Cloister Garden.

that faces us all in this global 21st century. Abbot Philip has commented, "if we can't learn to respect each other in this monastic environment of Christian love, there is no hope for the world." This is the same challenge of hope that Mohandas Gandhi put before us: to find God in the next person we meet. The international community of Christ in the Desert, and the love the brothers express to each other and to the friends whom they welcome to share in their spiritual life, has shown us that we do, indeed, have reason to hope.

The Community at Christ in the Desert, 1999.

❧ Past and Present Monks at Christ in the Desert 1964 – 2005
(List includes only professed monks)

Family Name, Monastic Name

Wall, Aelred
Cranor, Bernard*
McGough, Xavier*
Tran Van Thu, Mayeul*
Lawrence, Philip*
Leinenweber, John
Gardner, Christopher
Philen, Simon
Heath, Cassian
Leisy, Christian*
Sedillo, Aelred
Hogg, Leander*
Henderson, Michael
Koehler, Jeremy
Squire, Aelred
Cumberland, Francisco
Lemieux, André*
Whitmore, Paul
Regalado, Luis*
Vuong Luu Thien, PaulLavang*
Nguyen An Dzung, Andrew*
Comerzan, Paul
Nguyen Duc Hanh, Dominic*
Eco, Caedmon*

Alanis Rios, Francisco*
Vieira, Rafael
Matthiesen, Francis
Canonigo, Vicente
Nidea, Peter
Toyos Padres, Bartolome
Catajoy, Jacob
Fox, Mario
Lopez, Hugh*
Merino Flores, Antonio Manuel
Aparicio Salvador, Bartolome
Magaña García, Mauro
Sánchez Arriaga, Cesareo de Arles
Barrenechea Gonzales, Rodrigo*
Harmen, Nathanael
Varickamamthotty, Benedict
Ramos, John
Valencia, Esteban*
Huthmacher, Isaac
Vicente, Joseph
Nguven Van Tho, Odon*
Woytavich, William*
Martinez Sierra, Gabriel
Kneeland, Inigo

Cusimano, Joseph Gabriel* Montoya Salinas, Juan Manuel
Coelho, Jude Benitez Sánchez, Jose Maria*
Sequiera, Gerard* Pilarca, Lawrence*
Martinez, Francis Randall, Michael

*Currently resident

List of People Interviewed

Andronico Gallegos, Gallina, NM
Alex Gallegos, Española, NM
Karl Bode, Abiquiú, NM
Chris Chavez (USFS), Santa Fe, NM
Martha Yates (Archaeologist), La Madera, NM
Friedl Lang, Santa Fe, NM
Bob Trujillo, Abiquiú, NM
Roberta Brosseau, Santa Fe, NM
Daniel T. Kelly, Santa Fe, NM
Fr. James Connor (Fr. Tarcisius), Trappist, KY
Brother Edward Shivell, Mepkin, SC (letter)
James Koehler (Brother Jeremy), Santa Fe, NM
Sister Mary Benedicta Serna, CiD
Sister Julianne Allen, CiD
Brother Christian Leisy, CiD
Charles LoBianco (Brother Anthony), Millington, TN (letter)
Philippe Register, Santa Fe, NM
Brother Luis Regalado, CiD
Brother Bernard Cranor, CiD
Abbot Philip Lawrence, CiD
Alex Downs (Paleontologist, Ghost Ranch), Abiquiú, NM
Robert and Priscilla Bunker, Chacon, NM
Jane Serna, Española, NM
Florence Ault, Pojoaque, NM

✑ *Bibliography*

Aldrich, Hope. "Breaking the Sounds of Silence," *Santa Fe Reporter* (October 2, 1991).

Allen, John L. "Monks Target Catholic Slice of On-Line Market," *National Catholic Reporter* (April 17, 1998).

Aprile, Dianne. *The Abbey of Gethsemeni: Place of Peace and Paradox* (Louisville, KY: Trout Lily Press, 1998).

Barnes, Flo. "Finding the Sacred in Hospitality," *The New Mexican* (December30, 2001).

Blumenthal, E.H. Jr. "An Introduction to Gallina Archaelogy," *New Mexico Anthropologist* 4(1):10-13. (1940).

Buchanan, John. "A Place of Trial and Hope," *The Denver Post* (December 25, 1966).

Callaway, Larry. "Tradition-Bound Monastery Looks to Future." *Albuquerque Journal* (February 6, 1983).

Catholic Encyclopedia, The. Robert C. Broderick, ed. (Nashville, TN: Thomas Nelson, Inc., 1987).

Catholic Transcript, The. (May, 1963). Contains a discussion of Thomas Merton's impressions of the West and specifically New Mexico.

Christ in the Desert Monastery. "Abbot's Notebook" (2000-2005) www.christdesert. org..

_____. "Newsletters" (1964-2005).

Clabaigh, Colman. "Introduction to Monastic History," Monastic Formators Programme. Unpublished manuscript (Rome, 2004).

Claffey, Margaret. Unpublished notes on T. D. Burns. Christ in the Desert archives (no date).

Cleary, Edward L. *Crisis and Change: The Church in Latin America Today* (Maryknoll, NY: Orbis Books, 1985).

Cohen, Elizabeth. "Progress and the Pilgrims." *Ventana* (January, 1997).

Connor, James (Father Tarciscius). "The Monastery of Christ in the Desert: A Personal Report," *Monastic Exchange* (Winter, 1973-74).

Dula, Rodolfo E. "Brothers from Far and Near," *Malaya* (April 23, 1991).

Easthouse, Keith. "In Desert Calm, a Search for God," *The New Mexican* (September 20, 1992).

Ebright, Malcolm. *Land Grants and Lawsuits in Northern New Mexico.* New Mexico Land Grant Series, John R. Ness, ed. (Albuquerque, NM: University of New Mexico Press, 1994).

Elias, Jaffa. "Bön and Benedictine: A Relationship Buds," *Mandala* (September-November, 2002).

Evans, Illtud. "Religious Orders and Renewal," *The Tablet* (December 16. 1961).

Flynn, D. M. "Unfailing Treasures: Gregorian Chant and Spirituality," *Review for Religious* (November-December, 1999).

Flynn, Kathy. "Sister Turns Energies Toward Fundraising," *The New Mexican* (July 14, 1991).

Fritz, Craig. "Building on a Philosophy," *The New Mexican* (April 19, 1998).

"Funds Vital for Monastic Way of Living near Abiquiú," *Albuquerque Journal North* (December 25, 1991).

Gelineau, Joseph. *The Psalms—A New Translation* (Philadelphia: The Westminster Press, 1963).

_____. *Twenty-Four Psalms and a Canticle* (Chicago: GIA Publication, no date).

Gregory, (Pope). *Life and Miracles of Saint Benedict* (Collegeville, Minnesota: The Liturgical Press, no date).

Henao, Juliana. "El Abogado de los Indohispanos." *The New Mexican* (June 6, 2005).

Hibben, Frank. "The Gallina Phase," *American Antiquity* 14(2):131-136 (1938).

Hoffmann, Kathelyn. *The Legend of the Town of San Joaquin del Rio Chama* (Santa Fe, NM: Synergelic Press, 1983).

Hogg, Brother Leander. "The Visit of the Abbot of Menri to the Monastery of Christ in the Desert," *Monastic Interreligious Dialogue* (November 4, 2004). www.monasticdialog.com.

_____. "Tibetan Bön Monks at Christ in the Desert." Monastic Interreligious Dialogue Bulletin 66 (February, 2001) www.monasticdialog.com.

Illustrated History of New Mexico, An (Chicago: Lewis, 1895), p.645.

Knight, Al. "A Desert Encounter with Saint Benedict," *Rocky Mountain News* (December 3, 1978).

Kozikowski, Janusz. "Advent: A Season of Waiting," *The New Mexican* (December 23, 1973).

Kusel, Denise. "Sister Seeking Solitude Found Community in Need of Her Care," *The New Mexican* (July 21, 2004).

Le Meé, Katherine. *The Benedictine Gift to Music* (New York/Mahwah, NJ: The Paulist Press, 2003).

Levi, Peter. *The Frontiers of Paradise: A Study of Monks and Monasteries* (New York: Weidenfeld and Nicholson, 1987).

MacGregor, John. "Benedictines Construct," *The New Mexican* (September 11, 1966).

Mathews, Kay. "Rio Chama," *Wildwater: Rivers and Lands of the Southwest*, v.7, no.3 (June/July, 1986).

McCann, Justin. *Saint Benedict* (London: Sheed and Ward, 1979).

Merton, Thomas. *Dancing in the Water of Life* (San Francisco: HarperCollins, 1998).

_____. *Faith and Violence: Christian Teaching and Christian Practice* (Notre Dame, IN: University of Notre Dame Press, 1968)

_____. *The Asian Journal* (New York: New Directions, 1968).

_____. *Wisdom of the Desert* (New York: New Directions, 1970).

_____. *Woods, Shore, and Desert* (Albuquerque: University of New Mexico Press, 1963). Reissued by Museum of New Mexico Press. Santa Fe, NM, 1982.

Museum of New Mexico. "Newsletter" (October, 1966).

Nabokov, Peter. *Tijerina and the Courthouse Raid* (Berkeley, CA: The Ramparts Press, 1970).

Necker, Thomas. *Chama River Canyon Wilderness Guide*. United States Department of Agriculture, Santa Fe National Forest (no date.)

"Necrology," *Old Santa Fe*. Obituary of T. D. Burns (April, 1916) p.180.

New American Bible. Saint Joseph edition. (New York: Catholic Book Publishing Co., 1997).

Oakes, Edward T. "The Psalms as Christian Prayer," *America* (March 14, 1992).

Poling-Kempes, Lesley. *Valley of the Shining Stone* (Tucson: University of Arizona Press, 1997).

Psalms, The. Grail Translation. (Chicago: G.I.A. Publications, 1983).

Quintana, Frances Leon. *Pobladores: Hispanic Americans of the Ute Frontier*. Revised edition. (Frances Leon Quintana, 1991).

"Return to Saint Benedict," *Liturgical Arts* (September, 1965).

Rule of Saint Benedict in English, The. Timothy Fry, ed. (Collegeville, Minnesota: The Liturgical Press, 1982).

Roarke, J. Madeleva. *Father Damasus and the Founding of Mount Saviour* (Pine City, NY: madroar press, 1998).

Shannon, James P. "Thomas Merton's New Mexico," *New Mexico Magazine*, v.49, no.5-6 (May/June, 1971).

Sharpe, Tom. "Ground Cleared for Twenty-two Monks' Cells at Monastery," *Albuquerque Journal North* (January 11, 1994).

"Siemans Technology Powers Largest Private Solar Installation in New Mexico," *Siemans Scope* (April 19, 1998).

Simmons, Marc. "Bookseller Recalls Day with Georgia O'Keeffe in her Library," *The New Mexican* (May 28, 2005).

_____. *Witchcraft in the Southwest* (Lincoln, NE: University of Nebraska Press, 1974).

Skinner, Olivia. "Prior of a Monastery in New Mexico," *Saint Louis Post Dispatch* (October 31, 1968).

Smith, Craig. "Eternal Light, Eternal Chant," *The New Mexican* (*Pasatiempo*, October 17-23, 1997).

Stuart, D. E. and R. P. Gautier. *Prehistoric New Mexico*. State Planning Division, Historic Preservation Bureau, Department of Finance and Administration (Santa Fe, NM, 1981).

Tijerina, Reies Lopez. *They Called Me "Tiger"* (Houston, TX: Arte Publico Press, 2000).

Tipton, Nancy. "At the Keyboard, Religiously," *Albuquerque Journal* (August 29, 1995).

Torres, Robert. "'El Bornes': La Tierra Amarilla and T. D. Burns," *New Mexico Historical Review*, 56:2 (April, 1981).

Twitchell, Ralph. *The Leading Facts of New Mexico History*, v.5 (Cedar Rapids, IA: Torch Press, 1911).

"Voice in the Wilderness," *Albuquerque Journal Magazine* (July 4, 1978).

Walker, Hollis. "Our Lady of the Desert Monastery," *The New Mexican* (June 13, 1999).